BIBLE CENTERED CROSSWORDS

BIBLE CENTERED CROSSWORDS

Donovan A. Epp

BAKER BOOK HOUSE
Grand Rapids, Michigan 49516

Copyright © 1988 by Baker Books
a division of Baker Book House Company
P.O. Box 6287, Grand Rapids, MI 49516-6287

ISBN: 0-8010-3201-6

Ninth printing, June 1995

The King James Version of the Bible
is the reference for puzzles unless otherwise noted.

Printed in the United States of America

Your loving support made this book possible

1

Across

1. ___ was a tiller of the ground. (Gen. 4:2)
5. Thou shouldest put him in prison ___ in the stocks. (Jer. 29:26)
8. Slain by his brother. (Gen. 4:8)
12. Of the lily family. (Prov. 7:17)
13. ___ not to one another. (Col. 3:9)
14. Greek letter.
15. Containing NO_2 (comb. form).
16. Poe's "The Bottle ___."
17. Rodent (pl.).
18. Slowly, in music.
20. And the ark rested . . . upon the mountains of ___. (Gen. 8:4)
22. Bring to pass his ___, his strange ___. (Isa. 28:21)
23. The ___ of Aaron. (Num. 17:8)
24. The border was drawn to ___. (Josh.15:9)
27. Thomas, one of the ___. (John 20:24)
31. Bore his ear through with an ___. (Exod. 21:6, NIV)
32. Hin of ___. (Ezek. 45:24)
33. Deceive.
37. Stuffed to capacity.
40. The ___ was risen upon the earth when Lot entered into Zoar. (Gen. 19:23)
41. Son of Bela. (1 Chron. 7:7)
42. Pursues.
45. Barnabas a ___, and of the country of Cyprus. (Acts 4:36)
49. David himself followed the ___, (2 Sam. 3:31)
50. He casteth forth his ___ like morsels. (Ps. 147:17)
52. God's garden. (Gen. 2:8)
53. Spindle.
54. District of south-western India.
55. Rotary press print.
56. Legendary British king.
57. Cain went out from the presence of the LORD and dwelt in the land of ___. (Gen. 4:16)
58. In their anger they ___ a man. (Gen. 49:6)

Down

1. And the third day there was a marriage in ___. (John 2:1)
2. What Jehoida bored a hole in [2 words]. (2 Kings 12:9)
3. Small amount.
4. The men of Cuth made ___. (2 Kings 17:30)
5. Star of the Big Dipper.
6. Steal.
7. ___, and go in peace. (Acts 16:36)
8. Erode.
9. Thy servant slew both the lion and the ___. (1 Sam. 17:36)
10. Evangelical Teacher Training Association (abbr.).
11. Many that are first shall be ___. (Matt. 19:30)
19. International Cooperation Administration (abbr.).
21. Put pure frankincense upon each ___. (Lev. 24:7)
24. But cast the ___ away. (Matt. 13:48)
25. My heart standeth in ___ of thy word. (Ps. 119:161)
26. Yet have I made myself servant unto ___. (1 Cor. 9:19)
28. And one ___ of oil. (Lev. 14:10)
29. Contend.
30. Old times.
34. Thou shalt not be to him as an ___. (Exod. 22:25)
35. In ___ time Christ died. (Rom. 5:6)
36. As an ___ on an hill. (Isa. 30:17)
37. Is there no balm in ___? (Jer. 8:22)
38. Mineral containing metal.
39. Like a tree planted by the ___. (Ps. 1:3)
42. Thou shalt put the blessing upon mount Gerizim, and the curse upon mount ___. (Deut. 11:29)
43. Female water sprite.

1	2	3	4		5	6	7		8	9	10	11
12					13				14			
15					16				17			
18				19			20	21				
			22				23					
24	25	26					27			28	29	30
31										32		
33			34	35	36		37	38	39			
			40				41					
42	43	44					45			46	47	48
49					50	51			52			
53					54				55			
56					57				58			

44. From ___ to the wilderness. (Isa. 16:1)
46. Woe to the ___ shepherd that leaveth the flock! (Zech. 11:17, KJV)
47. ___-a-tete.
48. Enough.
51. Dove sound.

2

Across

1. The ___ number of them is to be redeemed. (Num. 3:48)
4. Pekod and ___ and Koa. (Ezek. 23:23)
8. Jonathan arose from the table in fierce anger, and did eat no ___. (1 Sam. 20:34)
12. Old card game.
13. Wither as the green ___. (Ps. 37:2)
14. Volcano in Sicily.
15. The heavens ___ the glory of God. (Ps. 19:1)
17. White (French).
18. Redeeming the ___, because the days are evil. (Eph. 5:16)
19. Son of Cush. (Gen. 10:7)
20. The plague of the ___, of the mule, of the camel, and of the ass. (Zech. 14:15)
22. ___ not unto thine own understanding. (Prov. 3:5)
23. Exclude.
24. And the curse upon mount ___. (Deut. 11:29)
25. Greek letter.
28. Have their ___ exercised. (Heb. 5:14)
30. The Father of ___, with whom is no variableness. (James 1:17)
32. How long will it be ___ ye make an end of words? (Job 18:2)
33. And ___ begat Aminidab. (Matt. 1:4)
35. Iranian monetary unit.
36. Conflict.
37. Ship's hull.
38. Soothe.
41. Descendant of Pharez. (1 Chron. 9:4)
42. Or ever I was ___. (Song of Sol. 6:12)
43. Something to be ___. (Phil. 2:6, NIV)
46. Descendant of Merari. (1 Chron. 24:27)
47. Of the alimentary canal.
48. Garden vegetable.
49. Formerly Persia.
50. Melody.
51. No room for them in the ___. (Luke 2:7)

Down

1. ___ things are passed away. (2 Cor. 5:17)
2. Hind.
3. Carried about with every wind of ___. (Eph. 4:14)
4. Counted worthy to suffer ___. (Acts 5:41)
5. He is risen; he is not ___. (Mark 16:6)
6. Mineral containing metal.
7. Jewish month.
8. Dark (comb. form).
9. Dwelt in the top of the rock ___. (Judg. 15:8)
10. Daughter of Phanuel. (Luke 2:36)
11. Indicates RPMs.
16. Registers.
17. Call me no more ___. (Hos. 2:16)
19. The ___ of the Chaldeans. (Dan. 9:1)
20. Stockings.
21. According to his eating, an ___ for every man. (Exod. 16:16)
22. Pound (abbr.).
24. Aram's father. (Matt. 1:3)
25. Macedonian city. (Acts 16:12)
26. Hart.
27. I John . . . was in the ___ that is called Patmos. (Rev. 1:9)
29. Enlarge thy baldness as the ___. (Mic. 1:16)
31. Beams.
34. Making them ___ ensample. (2 Peter 2:6)
36. ___ the saint of the LORD. (Ps. 106:16)
37. City of Judah. (2 Sam. 6:2)
38. Disciple of Babism.

39. Pitcher
40. The beginning of miracles, did Jesus in ___. (John 2:11)
41. Cereal.
43. Wildebeest.
44. Even (poet.).

45. Those that were numbered of them even of the tribe of ___. (Num. 1:39)
47. For I was envious ___ the foolish. (Ps. 73:3)

9

3

Across

1. Son of Shem. (Gen. 10:22)
4. Owned the legendary golden touch.
9. Of the crow family.
12. Anger.
13. Worship the golden ___. (Dan. 3:5)
14. Office of Price Administration (abbr.).
15. And the swan, and the ___ and the gier eagle. (Lev. 11:18)
17. Their wine is the poison of dragons and the cruel ___ of asps. (Deut. 32:33)
19. Duke Magdiel, duke ___. (1 Chron. 1:54)
20. From ___ to the wilderness. (Isa. 16:1)
21. Then Eliezer the son of Do- ___. (2 Chron. 20:37)
23. Succession of Pharaohs.
26. And the LORD God planted a garden eastward in ___. (Gen. 2:8)
27. The ___, a topaz. (Rev. 21:20)
28. Egyptian sun-god.
29. Industrial Engineering Research (abbr.).
30. Kind of cabbage.
31. Tribe of Manas- ___ were thirty and two thousand and two hundred. (Num. 1:35)
32. Tin symbol.
33. Targeted.
34. I will ___ thee out of my mouth. (Rev. 3:16, AMP)
35. Even the sea ___ (sing.) draw out the breast. (Lam. 4:3)
37. The latter end is ___. (2 Peter 2:20)
38. Current incurable disease.
39. Hindu woman's garment.
40. Houston baseball player.
42. Rehoboam . . . built cities for ___. (2 Chron. 11:5)
45. Princes eat in ___ season. (Eccles. 10:17)
46. Complain.
48. Destroy the inside of.
49. Mythological wife of Saturn.
50. Opposite of zenith.
51. Time period (abbr.).

Down

1. They shoot out the ___. (Ps. 22:7)
2. Suffix meaning function.
3. But ___ us from evil. (Matt. 6:13)
4. ___ the Morasthite prophesied in the days of Hezekiah. (Jer. 26:18)
5. Mosque prayer leader.
6. The rest of the children of Kohath had by lot out of . . . the tribe of ___. (Josh. 21:5)
7. Silver symbol.
8. The Lord appointed other ___ also. (Luke 10:1)
9. There shall no sign be given to it, but the sign of the prophet ___. (Matt. 12:39)
10. Prefix meaning separate.
11. Sweet potato.
16. Formerly Persia.
18. The sword of Goliath . . . whom thou slewest in the valley of ___. (1 Sam. 21:9)
20. Ecclesiastical council.
21. Natural religion based on human reason.
22. Gland (comb. form).
23. Aquatic athlete.
24. ___ of the field shall clap. (Isa. 55:12)
25. ___-h, Jehovah.
27. Your ___ are written in heaven. (Luke 10:20)
30. Many . . . shall ___[2 words] with Abraham. (Matt. 8:11)
31. Under the ___ of Pisgah. (Deut. 4:49)
33. Saudi Arabian principality.
34. With a ___ botch that cannot be healed. (Deut. 28:35)
36. Buttocks.

37. One unleavened ___ and shall put them upon the hands of the Nazarite. (Num. 6:19)

39. Six (Lat.).

40. Why make ye this ___, and weep? (Mark 5:39)

41. I will ___ with him and he with me. (Rev. 3:20)

42. The rulers knew not . . . what I ___. (Neh. 2:16)

43. Signal.

44. And so forth.

47. He saith among the trumpets, ___. (Job 39:25)

4

Across

1. For the ___ made nothing perfect. (Heb. 7:19)
4. All that pass by ___ their hands at thee. (Lam. 2:15)
8. She dwelleth and abideth . . . upon the ___ of the rock. (Job 39:28)
12. Father of Josaphat. (Matt. 1:8)
13. Lest he ___ thee to the judge. (Luke 12:58)
14. Ye that love the Lord, ___ evil. (Ps. 97:10)
15. Only the gold . . . the iron, the ___ and the lead. (Num. 31:22)
16. This house was finished on the third day of the month ___. (Ezra 6:15)
17. ___. Even so, come, Lord Jesus. (Rev. 22:20)
18. They shall even fall into the mouth of the ___. (Nah. 3:12)
20. Thou wast altogether born in ___. (John 9:34)
22. Thine ___ shall be clearer than the noonday. (Job 11:17)
24. Epistle.
28. He that ___ his rod hateth his son. (Prov. 13:24)
32. ___ [2 words] fools for Christ's sake. (1 Cor. 4:10)
33. And her ___ was to light on a part of the field. (Ruth 2:3)
34. Every ___ at that which is before her. (Amos 4:3)
36. Sibling, dim.
37. Aquila's previous address. (Acts 18:2)
40. The lion is come up from his ___. (Jer. 4:7)
43. And Jacob called the name of the place ___. (Gen. 32:30)
45. Benjamite town. (1 Chron. 8:12)
46. Looking diligently lest any man ___ of the grace of God. (Heb. 12:15)
48. And the people ___ upon him in the gate. (2 Kings 7:17)
52. Go ___ thyself within thine house. (Ezek. 3:24)

55. ___ that man and have no company with him. (2 Thess. 3:14)
57. Unit of energy.
58. Ah, I will ___ me of mine adversaries. (Isa. 1:24)
59. Let me be weighed in an ___ balance. (Job 31:6)
60. How long will it be ___ thou be quiet? (Jer. 47:6)
61. Certain porter. (Ezra 2:42)
62. I am not the Christ, but that I am ___ before him. (John 3:28)
63. Brother of Zechariah and Jaaziel. (1 Chron. 15:18)

Down

1. Even of ___ my people is risen up as an enemy. (Mic. 2:8)
2. Because he would not spend the time in ___. (Acts 20:16)
3. Your abundance may be a supply for their ___. (2 Cor. 8:14)
4. I ___ thee before God and the Lord Jesus Christ. (1 Tim. 5:21)
5. Nevertheless a ___ saw them and told Absalom. (2 Sam. 17:18)
6. ___, who shall live when God doeth this! (Num. 24:23)
7. Shall tribulation or distress . . . or ___ or sword? (Rom. 8:35)
8. While they behold your ___ conversation coupled with fear. (1 Peter 3:2)
9. It is a ___ of consecration. (Exod. 29:22)
10. They . . . ___ the sacrifices of the dead. (Ps. 106:28)
11. O.T. book (abbr.).
19. The young asses that ___ the ground shall eat. (Isa. 30:24)
21. A ___ commandment I give unto you. (John 13:34)
23. And so forth.
25. Ye shall not minish ought from your bricks of your daily ___. (Exod. 5:19)
26. Amerindian people.

27. My presence shall go with thee and I will give thee ___. (Exod. 33:14)
28. And entering into a ___ of Adramyttium we launched. (Acts 27:2)
29. His violent dealing shall come down upon his own ___. (Ps. 7:16)
30. In ___ [2 words] it shall be made with oil. (Lev. 6:21)
31. That the brass of it may be ___. (Ezek. 24:11)
35. ___ is like unto thee, O Lord among the Gods? (Exod. 15:11)
38. But thou O Lord art . . . the ___ up of mine head. (Ps. 3:3)
39. ___ brother, let me have joy of thee in the Lord. (Philem. 20)
41. I ask therefore for what ___ ye have sent for me? (Acts 10:29)

42. Hebrew measure. (Ezek. 45:14)
44. The ___ are fallen unto me in pleasant places. (Ps. 16:6)
47. ___ not the world, neither the things that are in the world. (1 John 2:15)
49. Rock named after a Midianite prince. (Judg. 7:25)
50. None is so fierce that ___ stir him up. (Job 41:10)
51. The house of ___. (Amos 1:5)
52. Dead or Red.
53. Gibus.
54. He shall be a vessel . . . meet for the master's ___. (2 Tim. 2:21)
56. Number of Absalom's murderers. (2 Sam. 18:15)

5

Across

1. If any be a hearer of the word, and not a ___. (James 1:23)
5. Harsh cry.
8. Greater love ___ no man than this. (John 15:13)
12. Woe to them that are at ___. (Amos 6:1)
13. ___ no man anything. (Rom. 13:8)
14. Level piece of ground.
15. For we ___ not against flesh and blood. (Eph. 6:12)
17. It will ___ him to powder. (Matt. 21:44)
18. They that count it pleasure to ___. (2 Peter 2:13)
19. Cake soaked in syrup.
20. Of your own selves shall men ___. (Acts 20:30)
22. Fiendish.
25. That ___ after the dust of the earth. (Amos 2:7)
26. Impulsive disciple.
27. Negative vote.
28. Lincoln.
29. Dims.
30. [David] feigned himself ___ in their hands. (1 Sam. 21:13)
31. Rubidium symbol.
32. Deadly.
33. Girl's name.
34. Sent to settle problems at Corinth.
36. Rubber.
37. Valuable minerals.
38. Question closely.
39. More prudent.
41. Coarse hairy plant.
44. Rare golf scores.
45. ___ alai.
46. Diminutive suffix.
47. I will give you ___. (Matt. 11:28)
48. Scrap of food.
49. Flightless South American bird.

Down

1. His favour is as ___ upon the grass. (Prov. 19:12)
2. All that handle the ___. (Ezek. 27:29)
3. From the Calabar bean.
4. ___ the devil. (James 4:7)
5. What do ye, loosing the ___? (Mark 11:5)
6. Stand in ___, and sin not. (Ps. 4:4)
7. ___ are of God. (1 John 5:19)
8. Refuge.
9. Heretical doctrines of 4th century Greek theologian.
10. ___ shall be found there. (Gen. 18:32)
11. [Judas] was a thief and ___ the bag. (John 12:6)
16. Upon the great ___ of their right foot. (Exod. 29:20).
17. Amusing activities.
19. Climbing pepper.
20. Come ye yourselves ___. (Mark 6:31)
21. They said unto him, ___, . . . where dwellest thou? (John 1:38)
22. Thou shalt not ___ to offer the first of thy ripe fruits. (Exod. 22:29)
23. Insubstantial.
24. Ancient biblical manuscript.
26. And thy ___ drop fatness. (Ps. 65:11)
29. Father (Lat.).
30. Unleavened bread eaten at Passover.
32. Asaph, the keeper of the king's ___. (Neh. 2:8)
33. They threw them into prison, charging the ___ to keep them safely. (Acts 16:23, RSV)
35. She called his name ___ . . . because I drew him out of the water. (Exod. 2:10)

36. To pull with effort.
38. Be strong and ___ yourselves like men. (1 Sam. 4:9)
39. When there falleth out any ___, they join also unto our enemies. (Exod. 1:10)
40. Blackish by reason of the ___. (Job 6:16)
41. I will break also the ___ of Damascus. (Amos 1:5)
42. Female saint (abbr.).
43. Am I a ___ or a whale? (Job 7:12)
45. Minor prophet (abbr.).

6

Across

1. Bristle of grass.
4. Coffin.
8. Turning (comb. form).
12. Debt.
13. Region.
14. Dramatic part.
15. To the only wise God be . . . ___ and power. (Jude 25)
17. So be it.
18. And it ___ worms and stank. (Exod. 16:20)
19. And ___ said unto God, If Thou wilt save Israel by mine hand. (Judg. 6:36)
21. Hebrew place of the dead.
23. I ___ on the work of thy hands. (Ps. 143:5)
24. ___ ye from your evil ways. (2 Kings 17:13)
25. Laborious.
29. Bravo!
30. Clergyman's residence.
31. A legal procedure.
32. Former Iranian ruler's title.
34. I have put a yoke of iron upon the ___. (Jer. 28:14)
35. Marvel not that I ___. (John 3:7)
36. Thin circular objects.
37. To search about.
40. Prefix meaning 'skill'.
41. Melody.
42. Imparter of knowledge.
46. Not (comb. form).
47. They shall say in all the highways ___. (Amos 5:16)
48. Did I ___ lightness? (2 Cor. 1:17)
49. Northeast elevation (abbr.)
50. Computer logic circuits.
51. Doctor of Sacred Theology.

Down

1. Assist.
2. Court.
3. Hairs of your head are all ___. (Matt. 10:30)
4. Jury.
5. Climate of the Gaza desert.
6. Astral constellation.
7. Haughty people of the earth do ___. (Isa. 24:4)
8. Barters.
9. I must also see ___. (Acts 19:21)
10. Margarine.
11. One of the thirteen original states (abbr.).
16. And the ___ did swim. (2 Kings 6:6)
20. Be still ye inhabitants of the ___. (Isa. 23:2)
21. ___ all wells of water. (2 Kings 3:19)
22. Polynesian dance.
23. Unit.
25. Polynesian language.
26. I beseech thee for my son ___, whom I have begotten in my bonds. (Philem. 1:10)
27. And they shall ___ him. (Mark 10:34)
28. Large deer.
30. Minnesota Scholastic Aptitude Exam (abbr.)
33. Thy name shall be called no more Jacob, but ___. (Gen. 32:28)
34. Containing NO_2 atoms (comb. form).
36. Purely purge away thy ___. (Isa. 1:25)
37. Satyr.
38. Eagle.
39. Thou hast caused men to ___ over our heads. (Ps. 66:12)
40. I will fetch my knowledge from ___. (Job 36:3)
43. National Labor Organization (abbr.)
44. Suffix for superlative degree.
45. West wind, which took away the locusts, and cast them into the ___ sea. (Exod. 10:19)

7

Across

1. The heron after her kind, and the lapwing, and the ___. (Lev. 11:19)
4. He spake, and commanded that they should ___ the furnace. (Dan. 3:19)
8. The tree of life which ___ twelve manner of fruits. (Rev. 22:2)
12. Now ___ the priest sat upon a seat by a post. (1 Sam. 1:9)
13. Large constellation.
14. Son of Seth. (Gen. 4:26)
15. Israelite judge/prophet (abbr.). (1 Sam. 3:19)
16. Nicolas, a ___ of Antioch. (Acts 6:5)
18. The ___ of Tema looked. (Job 6:19)
20. Salt.
21. But ___ the spirits whether they are of God. (1 John 4:1)
22. To begin with.
26. Monetary unit of Thailand.
28. My people are ___ to backsliding from me. (Hos. 11:7)
29. Water (French).
30. Liquor.
31. We should bring the firstfruits of our ___. (Neh. 10:37)
32. Outfit.
33. Son of Peleg. (Gen. 11:18)
34. Salvation unto the ___ of the earth. (Acts 13:47)
35. Volcano in Sicily.
36. Green algae.
38. Son of Caleb. (1 Chron. 4:15)
39. Distinctive doctrine.
40. Son of Jeroham. (1 Chron. 12:7)
43. If a man be ___ in a fault. (Gal. 6:1)
47. Meadow.
48. Herbaceous plant.
49. And next to them builded Zaccur the son of ___. (Neh. 3:2)
50. Geber the son of ___ was in the country of Gilead. (1 Kings 4:19)
51. Goliath the Philistine, whom thou slewest in the valley of ___. (1 Sam. 21:9)
52. Record.
53. Musical syllable.

Down

1. Bring forth the ___ robe. (Luke 15:22)
2. Winged.
3. Paul's workfellow. (Rom. 16:21)
4. ___ is he that hath the God of Jacob. (Ps. 146:5)
5. Sins.
6. Achaia was ready a year ___. (2 Cor. 9:2)
7. I am full of ___ to and fro. (Job 7:4)
8. They made ___ of pure gold. (Exod. 39:25)
9. The Lord is . . . not willing that ___ should perish. (2 Peter 3:9)
10. He chooseth a tree that will not ___. (Isa. 40:20)
11. Compass point.
17. The ___ was without form. (Gen. 1:2)
19. Scrap of food.
22. Vendettas.
23. A certain orator, named ___, who informed the governor against Paul. (Acts 24:1)
24. He had ___ in the grave four days. (John 11:17)
25. Hindu world cycle age.
26. Poet.
27. Windward side.
28. Abraham had two sons, the one by a ___. (Gal. 4:22)
31. Infidel.
35. How long will it be ___ thou be quiet. (Jer. 47:6)
37. I will prove thee with ___. (Eccles. 2:1)

	1	2	3		4	5	6	7		8	9	10	11
12					13					14			
15					16				17				
18				19				20					
			21				22				23	24	25
26	27				28					29			
30				31						32			
33				34					35				
36			37				38						
			39				40				41	42	
43	44	45			46				47				
48				49					50				
51				52					53				

38. Ancient Greek dialect.
40. Jersey (abbr.).
41. Aviation (comb. form).
42. I will cause it to rain a very grievous ___. (Exod. 9:18)

43. ___ no man any thing. (Rom. 13:8)
44. ___ -au-vent, meat pie.
45. Epoch.
46. Korean military intelligence (abbr.).

19

8

Across

1. When ___ was dead, behold an angel of the Lord appeareth. (Matt. 2:19)
6. Herod's brother. (Matt. 14:3)
12. Synthetic polymer.
14. Lowland (Scot.).
15. Musical syllable.
16. Riches perish by evil ___. (Eccles. 5:14)
18. Tossed ___ and fro, and carried about. (Eph. 4:14)
19. The serpent beguiled ___ through his subtilty. (2 Cor. 11:3)
21. Belonging to them.
22. Come down ___ my child die. (John 4:49)
23. Gambles.
25. Girl's name.
26. Descant.
27. Most recent.
29. Bric-a- ___.
30. ___ Hashanah, Jewish New Year.
31. All our righteousnesses are as filthy ___. (Isa. 64:6)
32. And to Seth to him also there was born a son . . . ___. (Gen. 4:26)
33. Lost his vineyard. (1 Kings 21:1)
35. Enthusiasm.
36. Woman, behold thy ___. (John 19:26)
37. Float.
39. Nothing.
40. Vice ___.
42. ___ Paulo, Brazil.
43. Bone.
44. Rapid vibration of a musical tone.
46. Ruthenium (symbol).
47. Orator.
49. The son of man whom thou ___ strong for thyself. (Ps. 80:17)
51. Parrots.
52. A sharp rock . . . the name of the other ___. (1 Sam. 14:4)

Down

1. And came to the mountain of God, even to ___. (Exod. 3:1)
2. Peter standing up with the ___. (Acts 2:14)
3. With regard to.
4. Do ye, as ___ as ye drink it. (1 Cor. 11:25)
5. Whose waters cast up mire and ___. (Isa. 57:20)
6. Lead me in a ___ path. (Ps. 27:11).
7. John was clothed with camel's ___. (Mark 1:6)
8. Love worketh no ___. (Rom. 13:10)
9. Lending library (abbr.).
10. Healing (comb. form).
11. Breath (comb. form).
13. Then ___ the Ammonite came up and encamped. (1 Sam. 11:1)
17. Wine which hath no ___. (Job 32:19)
20. The gift of God is ___ life. (Rom. 6:23)
22. ___ the chamberlain of the city saluteth you. (Rom. 16:23)
24. The sucklings ___ in the streets. (Lam. 2:11)
26. To him also pertains the region of ___. (1 Kings 4:13)
28. Alphabet letter.
29. ___ el Mandeb, strait.
31. I will ___ them from the power of the grave. (Hos. 13:14)
32. So the waters were healed . . . according to the saying of ___. (2 Kings 2:22)
33. Standard.
34. Grating.
35. ___-mous, huge.
36. Then shall the ___ be ashamed. (Mic. 3:7)
38. Let no man despise thy ___. (1 Tim. 4:12)
40. Afrikaner woman.
41. ___! for that day is great. (Jer. 30:7)

44. (Evangelical) Teaching Training
    Association (abbr.)
45. Canticle.
48. Habitat (comb. form).
50. Within (prefix).

9

Across

1. The time is ___ passed. (Mark 6:35)
4. Son of Bichri. (2 Sam. 20:1)
9. Every knee should ___. (Phil. 2:10)
12. ___ no man anything. (Rom. 13:8)
13. Not that other men be ___. (2 Cor. 8:13)
14. Son of Jether. (1 Chron. 7:38)
15. Spurns.
17. Ten ___ of vineyard shall yield one bath. (Isa. 5:10)
19. Neither by any other ___. (James 5:12)
20. So be it.
21. Hymn writer, Philip Paul ___.
23. Lintel.
26. Milk (comb. form).
27. Except I shall see in his hands the ___ of the nails. (John 20:25)
28. This ___ in remembrance of me. (1 Cor. 11:24)
29. Fruit drink.
30. All the brethren ___ you. (1 Cor. 16:20)
31. Dove sound.
32. All ye shall be offended because of ___. (Mark 14:27)
33. How that in a great ___ of affliction. (2 Cor. 8:2)
34. ___ profane and vain babblings. (2 Tim. 2:16)
35. I will cause the enemy to ___ thee. (Jer. 15:11)
37. The Cretians are alway ___. (Tit. 1:12)
38. Quantity of paper.
39. Roll up.
40. A great ___ knit at the four corners. (Acts 10:11)
42. Manages.
45. Legume.
46. Flowering shrub.
48. Mineral containing metal.
49. Suffer little children, ___ forbid them not, to come. (Matt. 19:14)
50. For childhood and ___ are vanity. (Eccles. 11:10)
51. Alighted.

Down

1. They shall be heard ___ their much speaking. (Matt. 6:7)
2. Stand in ___, and sin not. (Ps. 4:4)
3. My lips shall greatly ___. (Ps. 71:23)
4. The Sadducees and Essenes.
5. ___ the rain a father? (Job 38:28)
6. Alphabet letter.
7. ___ ye not unwise. (Eph. 5:17)
8. Their hearts as an ___ stone. (Zech. 7:12)
9. So shall thy ___ be filled with plenty. (Prov. 3:10)
10. Swedish monetary unit.
11. And there ___ light. (Gen. 1:3)
16. Lot journeyed ___. (Gen. 13:11)
18. Penny.
20. Yet I will distress ___. (Isa. 29:2.)
21. Be holy and without ___ before him in love. (Eph. 1:4)
22. A people ___ with iniquity. (Isa. 1:4)
23. Minister to.
24. An ___ of a sweet smell. (Phil. 4:18)
25. Offerings, in the feasts and in the new ___. (Ezek. 45:17)
27. King of Troy.
30. And he pressed upon them ___. (Gen. 19:3)
31. Not as wise as Solomon. (1 Kings 4:31)
33. The ___ of life. (Gen. 2:9)
34. Father.
36. Power to ___ on serpents. (Luke 10:19)
37. Careen.
39. Decree.
40. Health resort.
41. As a ___ gathereth her chickens. (Matt. 23:37)
42. Dairymen's Labor Union (abbr.).
43. Three (comb. form).

44. I am ___ for the defence of the
    gospel. (Phil. 1:17)
47. Loved by Zeus.

10

Across

1. Make thee an ___ of gopherwood. (Gen. 6:14)
4. ___ was a just man and perfect in his generations. (Gen. 6:9)
8. Noah begat three sons, ___, Ham, and Japheth.
12. Red or Mediterranean.
13. Son of Pahathmoab. (Ezra 10:30)
14. Atmosphere (comb. form).
15. Relief.
16. The ___ of the house of David. (Isa. 22:22)
17. Wild goose.
18. Saul ___ David from that day and forward. (1 Sam. 18:9)
20. Who will make me a ___? (Job 24:25)
21. Inspected with intent to rob.
23. Heir.
26. Laughing sound.
27. And Huram made the ___. (2 Chron. 4:11)
28. ___ gave me of the tree. (Gen. 3:12)
29. Because in the night ___ of Moab is laid waste. (Isa. 15:1)
30. Arrives.
33. Tone of musical scale.
34. This is my beloved ___. (Matt. 3:17)
36. Hint.
37. Stylish.
39. Isolates.
41. Trespass.
42. ___! for that day is great. (Jer. 30:7)
43. They gave forth their ___. (Acts 1:26)
44. Gold coin.
46. Deer.
47. No man can serve ___ masters. (Matt. 6:24)
50. Ireland.
51. Evict.
52. One of the sons of Benjamin. (Gen. 46:21)
53. There was none that moved the ___. (Isa. 10:14)
54. Proceeds.
55. ___ -pros, legal maneuver.

Down

1. King of Judah. (2 Chron. 14:1)
2. Israelite loyal to David. (1 Kings 1:8)
3. They returned and came to Enmishpat, which is ___. (Gen. 14:7)
4. The eyes of them both were opened, and they knew that they were ___. (Gen. 3:7)
5. A prophet of the LORD was there, whose name was ___. (2 Chron. 28:9)
6. Not willing that ___ should perish. (2 Peter 3:9)
7. He saith among the trumpets ___. (Job 39:25)
8. ___ was barren, she had no child. (Gen. 11:30)
9. I will also vex the ___ of many people. (Ezek. 32:9)
10. Osprey.
11. Witty saying.
17. Anger (Scot.).
19. Continue there a ___, and buy and sell. (James 4:13)
20. River in Hades.
21. Five of you shall ___ an hundred. (Lev. 26:8)
22. They made the calf which ___ made. (Exod. 32:35)
23. Befuddle.
24. Electric level of resistance.
25. Hitler's empire.
27. Fades.
31. Brilliance.
32. Scotchman.
35. Nicotinic acid.
38. Who else can ___ hereunto? (Eccles. 2:25)

The grid (crossword puzzle):

1	2	3		4	5	6	7		8	9	10	11
12				13					14			
15				16				17				
	18	19				20						
21	22				23					24	25	
26				27					28			
29		30	31					32		33		
34		35		36				37	38			
39			40				41					
	42				43							
44	45			46					47	48	49	
50			51					52				
53			54					55				

40. David . . . took thence a stone and
    ___ it. (1 Sam. 17:49)
41. Bards.
43. And ___ thy sweet words. (Prov.
    23:8)
44. As the early ___ it goeth away.
    (Hos. 6:4)
45. I have called by name Bezaleel the
    son of ___. (Exod. 31:2)

46. Pair.
48. ___ is like unto thee, O LORD. (Exod.
    15:11)
49. Thou anointest my head with ___.
    (Ps. 23:5)
51. For only ___ king of Bashan
    remained of the remnant of giants.
    (Deut. 3:11)

11

Across

1. When he departed, he took out two ___. (Luke 10:35)
6. Canst thou mark when the hinds do ___? (Job 39:1)
11. Hebrew name for God.
13. Better is a ___ of herbs where love is. (Prov. 15:17)
14. Second tone of diatonic scale.
15. Emptiness.
17. Egyptian chief deity.
18. And Adam called his wife's name ___ because she was the mother of all living. (Gen. 3:20)
20. But all things ___ not. (1 Cor. 10:23)
21. My country ___ of thee.
22. Son of Jeduthun. (1 Chron. 25:3)
24. Gnome.
25. Even of ___ my people is risen up. (Mic. 2:8)
26. Of the sons of ___. (Ezra 10:43)
28. Mysteriously.
30. Ally tribe of Egypt. (Ezek. 30:4, 5)
32. Hindu queen.
33. Ancient Greek gold coin.
35. And straightway they forsook their ___. (Mark 1:18)
37. The children of the porters . . . the children of ___. (Ezra 2:42)
38. His master shall bore his ear through with an ___. (Exod. 21:6)
40. Flightless South American bird.
42. But we ___ the sentence of death in ourselves. (2 Cor. 1:9)
43. And Moses called ___ the son of Nun Jehoshua. (Num. 13:16)
45. Son of Benjamin. (Gen. 46:21)
46. Intravenous (abbr.).
47. Cheap.
49. Veterans Administration (abbr.).
50. Comes back.
52. City of Shechem. (Gen. 33:18)
54. The ___ be for the king's household to ride on. (2 Sam. 16:2)
55. Son of Gad. (Gen. 46:16)

Down

1. All the sons of ___ that dwelt at Jerusalem. (Neh. 11:6)
2. And he was numbered with the ___ apostles. (Acts 1:26)
3. Art thou better than populous ___. (Nah. 3:8)
4. Letter of Greek alphabet.
5. One (German).
6. Wilt thou judge the bloody ___? (Ezek. 22:2)
7. The Lord is . . . not willing that ___ should perish. (2 Peter 3:9)
8. Natural logarithm (sym.).
9. The works of his hands are ___ and judgment. (Ps. 111:7)
10. Expunge.
12. This is the man that ___ not God his strength. (Ps. 52:7)
13. For who maketh thee to ___ from another? (1 Cor. 4:7)
16. Egyptian river.
19. And he ___ there an altar. (Gen. 33:20)
21. He took the damsel by the hand and said . . . ___ cumi. (Mark 5:41)
23. Son of David. (2 Sam. 5:15)
25. Oceangoing vessel.
27. As of one born ___ of due time. (1 Cor. 15:8)
29. All the city was moved, and the people ___ together. (Acts 21:30)
31. Wherefore are we counted as ___. (Job 18:3)
33. Am I a dog, that thou comest to me with ___? (1 Sam. 17:43)
34. River joining the Rhine.
36. Worshipped and ___ the creature more than the Creator. (Rom. 1:25)
37. Son of Enan. (Num. 1:15)
39. Meadows.
41. City of Naphtali. (Josh. 19:33)
43. And let ___ also learn to maintain good works. (Tit. 3:14)

44. ___ -liah, daughter of Omri king of Israel (2 Kings 8:26)
47. Hint.
48. Give ___ to my words, O LORD. (Ps. 5:1)

51. Christian service (abbr.).
53. ___ I am come . . . to do thy will, O God. (Heb. 10:7)

12

Across

1. O ___ your hands, all ye people. (Ps. 47:1)
5. Essenes or Sadducees.
9. His mother's name also was ___, the daughter of Zachariah. (2 Kings 18:2)
12. Let them that ___ him be as the sun. (Judg. 5:31)
13. The sons of ___. (1 Chron. 7:12)
14. And I will . . . take away all thy ___. (Isa. 1:25)
15. Of the tribe of ___ were sealed twelve thousand. (Rev. 7:6)
16. In the land of Ephraim. (Judg. 12:15)
18. Compact.
20. The ___ and the bath shall be of one measure. (Ezek. 45:11)
21. Than for a rich man to enter ___ the kingdom of God. (Matt. 19:24)
24. At midnight Paul and ___ prayed and sang praises unto God. (Acts 16:25)
27. And Joelah and ___, the sons of Jeroham of Gedor. (1 Chron. 12:7)
31. Trigonometric function.
32. Nog.
33. Bristly, springy plant parts.
35. I took the little book . . . and ___ it up. (Rev. 10:10)
36. Be still ye inhabitants of the ___. (Isa. 23:2)
38. Unconcerned.
40. God trieth the hearts and ___. (Ps. 7:9)
42. Father of Salathiel. (Luke 3:27)
43. Increase.
45. That henceforth we should not ___ sin. (Rom. 6:6)
49. Holy and ___ is his name. (Ps. 111:9)
53. Faith that is in thee, which dwelt first in thy grandmother ___. (2 Tim. 1:5)
54. Spanish cheer.
55. ___ lama sabachthani? (Mark 15:34)
56. Anglo-saxon slave.
57. All therefore whatsoever they ___ you observe. (Matt. 23:3)
58. Who is this that cometh from Edom with ___ garments? (Isa. 63:1)
59. Judge.

Down

1. And was ___ with zeal as a cloke. (Isa. 59:17)
2. He that findeth his life shall ___ it. (Matt. 10:39)
3. Cut off the inhabitant from the plain of ___. (Amos 1:5)
4. The power of ___ and Media, the nobles and princes. (Esther 1:3)
5. The trees of the LORD are full of ___. (Ps. 104:16)
6. Son of Benjamin. (Gen. 46:21)
7. Wrap a dead body.
8. But they shall be snares and ___ unto you. (Josh. 23:13)
9. Daughter of King Omri. (2 Kings 8:26)
10. Written life history.
11. And brought him to an ___ and took care of him. (Luke 10:34)
17. O that they were wise, that they understood___. (Deut. 32:29)
19. Thou shouldst be for salvation unto the ___ of the earth. (Acts 13:47)
22. And they ___ unto it a lace of blue. (Exod. 39:31)
23. Made of certain grain.
25. Poker stake.
26. For his ___ remaineth in him. (1 John 3:9)
27. So Joram went over to ___ and all the chariots with him. (2 Kings 8:21)
28. Give me children or ___ I die. (Gen. 30:1)
29. Unless ye have ___ in vain. (1 Cor. 15:2)
30. I ___ and abhor lying: but thy law do I love. (Ps. 119:163)

34. And his ___ are open unto their prayers. (1 Peter 3:12)

37. Action or process (suffix).

39. And the greater house he ___ with fir tree. (2 Chron. 3:5)

41. And came and ___ them into the pot of pottage. (2 Kings 4:39)

44. Like a snakelike fish.

46. I am the ___ of Sharon. (Song of Sol. 2:1)

47. I will bewail with the weeping of Jazer the ___ of Sibmah. (Isa. 16:9)

48. ___ -plastic, having the power to unify different things.

49. And they ___ the threshingfloors. (1 Sam. 23:1)

50. They slew a bullock and brought the child to ___. (1 Sam. 1:25)

51. Until the day that ___ entered into the ark. (Matt. 24:38)

52. Who ___ no sin, neither was guile found in his mouth. (1 Peter 2:22)

13

Across

1. My sore ___ in the night. (Ps. 77:2)
4. Disciple of Babism.
8. ___ all that were pleasant to the eye. (Lam. 2:4)
12. Mother of Hezekiah. (2 Kings 18:2)
13. ___ for all the evil abominations. (Ezek. 6:11)
14. What ___ we to do with thee, Jesus? (Matt. 8:29)
15. Son of Jeconiah. (1 Chron. 3:18)
17. So be it.
18. And the ___ and kite, and the vulture after his kind. (Deut. 14:13)
19. Suffix meaning capable of.
21. Sell that ye have and give ___. (Luke 12:33)
24. Buy the truth and sell ___ [2 words]. (Prov. 23:23)
27. Absalom's hang-up.
30. Within as it were an half ___ of land. (1 Sam. 14:14)
32. ___ me and know my thoughts. (Ps. 139:23)
33. They ___ in vision, they stumble in judgment. (Isa. 28:7)
34. He is ___ before the sun. (Job 8:16)
35. Young asses that ___ the ground. (Isa. 30:24)
36. Son of Ephraim. (1 Chron. 7:27)
37. Talk irrationally.
38. Their words seemed to them as ___ tales. (Luke 24:11)
39. City of Naphtali. (Josh. 19:33)
41. With Zebadiah and Arad. (1 Chron. 8:15)
43. They made upon the ___ of the robe. (Exod. 39:24)
45. We roar all like bears and mourn sore like ___. (Isa. 59:11)
49. The threshingfloor of ___. (Gen. 50:10)
51. Thou ___ the year with thy goodness. (Ps. 65:11)
54. Gaddi the son of ___. (Num. 13:11)
55. Father of Kish. (2 Chron. 29:12)
56. International Association of Universities (abbr.).
57. Jewish measure.
58. Very pleasant hast thou ___ unto me. (2 Sam. 1:26)
59. Oshea the son of ___. (Num. 13:8)

Down

1. So that the earth ___ again. (1 Sam. 4:5)
2. And ___, he also brought of the firstlings of his flock. (Gen. 4:4)
3. Brood of pheasants.
4. Therefore is the name of it called ___; because the LORD did there confound the language. (Gen. 11:9)
5. ___ Baba and the forty thieves.
6. Sheep's bleat.
7. Thou shalt call me ___. (Hos. 2:16)
8. And thou ___ know the LORD. (Hos. 2:20)
9. We have mourned unto you and ye have not ___. (Matt. 11:17)
10. Beguiled by the serpent. (Gen. 3:13)
11. Sebaceous cyst.
16. Jewish month. (Esther 3:7)
20. ___ entendu (Fr.), well understood.
22. Call me not Naomi, call me ___. (Ruth 1:20)
23. One ___, a Jew and chief of priests. (Acts 19:14)
25. Verbal.
26. Herod was highly displeased with them of ___. (Acts 12:20)
27. City on the Euphrates. (2 Kings 19:13)
28. Of ___, the family of the Arodites. (Num. 26:17)
29. Son of Tehinnah. (1 Chron. 4:12)
31. A bruised ___ shall he not break. (Isa. 42:3)
34. Sinister.
38. ___ is taken out of the earth. (Job 28:2)

40. The power of Persia and ___. (Esther 1:3)
42. ___ Meese, former U.S. Attorney General.
44. The Lord will smite with a ___. (Isa. 3:17)
46. Surely there is a ___ for the silver. (Job 28:1)

47. The first came out red . . . and they called his name ___. (Gen. 25:25)
48. Amaze.
49. Suffix denoting enzymes.
50. Ram.
52. Relative biological effectiveness (abbr.).
53. Canticle.

14

Across

1. ___, the beloved physician, and Demas, greet you. (Col. 4:14)
5. The LORD ___ make thy thigh to rot. (Num. 5:21)
9. The sons of Elpaal . . . who built Ono and ___, with the towns thereof. (1 Chron. 8:12)
12. Thou shalt put the blessing upon mount Gerizim, and the curse upon mount ___. (Deut. 11:29)
13. And the burning ___, that shall consume the eyes. (Lev. 26:16)
14. The child did minister unto the LORD before ___ the priest. (1 Sam. 2:11)
15. Peculiarity.
17. A freewill offering in ___ or sheep. (Lev. 22:21)
19. He that hath ___ to hear, let him hear. (Matt. 11:15)
20. Cause it to be heard unto ___, O poor Anathoth. (Isa. 10:30)
21. He is the father of ___, the father of David. (Ruth 4:17)
23. Novelist, Hermann ___.
25. He planteth an ___, and the rain doth nourish it. (Isa. 44:14)
26. Son of Dishan. (Gen. 36:28)
28. Stand by the way and ___. (Jer. 48:19)
31. Alphabet letter.
32. To offer a great sacrifice unto ___ their god. (Judg. 16:23)
34. Musical syllable.
35. Who will make me a ___? (Job 24:25)
38. Ye shall in no ___ enter into the kingdom of heaven. (Matt. 5:20)
39. Buddy.
40. His ___ had offended their lord the king of Egypt. (Gen. 40:1)
42. Eighth foundation. (Rev. 21:20)
44. Hackneyed.
46. Ruin.
47. Rat or mouse.
49. And they dwelt in their ___ until the captivity. (1 Chron. 5:22)
52. And the king of Assyria brought men from Babylon . . . and from ___. (2 Kings 17:24)
53. The city of ___ father of Anak, which city is Hebron.
55. Skin blemishes.
56. The ___ of the scribes is in vain. (Jer. 8:8)
57. Enzyme (comb. form).
58. Coppice.

Down

1. Astral constellation.
2. Unger's Bible Dictionary (abbr.).
3. And pitched in the wilderness of Zin, which is ___. (Num. 33:36)
4. And if ye will receive it, this is ___. (Matt. 11:14)
5. For my ___ are vanity. (Job 7:16)
6. Giant king. (Num. 21:33)
7. Rustic boat.
8. Thou settest a print upon the ___. (Job 13:27)
9. Taxes.
10. Spanish cheers.
11. She brought forth butter in a lordly ___. (Judg. 5:25)
16. I give unto you power to ___ on serpents and scorpions. (Luke 10:19)
18. When thou wilt ___ thyself abroad. (Deut. 23:13)
21. Wife of Heber the Kenite. (Judg. 4:17)
22. Father of Naum. (Luke 3:25)
23. Sarah's handmaid. (Gen. 16:1)
24. Father of Cainan. (Gen. 5:9)
27. The ___ that is set before us. (Heb. 12:1)
29. ___ ye therefore the Lord of the harvest. (Matt. 9:38)
30. They shall ___ as lions' whelps. (Jer. 51:38)

Crossword Grid

1	2	3	4		5	6	7	8		9	10	11
12					13					14		
15				16			17		18			
		19							20			
21	22					23	24					
25				26	27				28		29	30
31				32				33			34	
35		36	37		38					39		
		40		41				42	43			
44	45					46						
47				48		49				50	51	
52			53		54		55					
56			57				58					

33. Father of Jeroboam. (1 Kings 11:26)
36. Son of Gideoni. (Num. 1:11)
37. Even after a certain ___ every day. (2 Chron. 8:13)
39. ___ the word; be instant in season. (2 Tim. 4:2)
41. Son of Eliphaz. (Gen. 36:11)
43. Also called Aeneas. (Acts 9:33)
44. Let their table be made a snare and a ___. (Rom. 11:9)

45. Wander.
46. Bachelor of Science in Agricultural Engineering (abbr.).
48. I will melt them and ___ them. (Jer. 9:7)
50. Deoxyribonucleic acid (abbr.).
51. A time to rend and a time to ___. (Eccles. 3:7)
54. Bachelor of Music (abbr.).

15

Across

1. Ye pay the tithe of mint and ___. (Matt. 23:23)
6. The ___ was in the ear and the flax was bolled. (Exod. 9:31)
12. Wilderness diet.
13. Give us seven days' ___ that we may send messengers. (1 Sam. 11:3)
14. Murdered by Joab. (2 Sam. 3:27)
15. Old English letter.
16. ___ I am warm, I have seen the fire. (Isa. 44:16)
17. ___ I am with you alway. (Matt. 28:20)
18. Loved this present world. (2 Tim. 4:10)
20. Growl.
21. Member of Old English alphabet.
23. Dollar (abbr.).
24. Take thou also unto thee wheat, and barley, and ___. (Ezek. 4:9)
25. Medieval Chinese ruler.
27. And the hail ___ throughout all the land of Egypt. (Exod. 9:25)
29. Lord, shall we ___ with the sword. (Luke 22:49)
31. They allure through the ___ of the flesh. (2 Peter 2:18)
34. Son of Merari. (Exod. 6:19)
36. Thy ___ and thy she goats have not cast their young. (Gen. 31:38)
38. Son of Nahash. (2 Sam. 17:27)
41. King of Midian. (Num. 31:8)
43. For the body is not ___ member but many. (1 Cor. 12:14)
44. Bel boweth down, ___ stoopeth. (Isa. 46:1)
45. Upright.
47. Saint (abbr.)
48. I knew a man in Christ above fourteen years ___. (2 Cor. 12:2)
49. Why make ye this ___, and weep? (Mark 5:39)
50. The Lord himself shall descend from heaven with a ___. (1 Thess. 4:16)
52. They ___ from the city, every man to his tent. (2 Sam. 20:22)
54. Turkish porter.
55. City of Judah. (Josh. 15:52)
56. Old.

Down

1. Son of Eliphaz. (Gen. 36:12)
2. Ahab stole ___ vineyard. (1 Kings 21:1)
3. There was no room for them in the ___. (Luke 2:7)
4. Trim (Scot.).
5. Shall bring down the heifer unto a rough valley, which is neither ___ nor sown. (Deut. 21:4)
6. Let them sing aloud upon their ___. (Ps. 149:5)
7. He planteth an ___, and the rain doth nourish it. (Isa. 44:14)
8. Relief pitcher (abbr.).
9. Climbing herbaceous vine.
10. Authored Psalm 89. (RSV)
11. We spend our ___ as a tale that is told. (Ps. 90:9)
13. The king thought to set him over the whole ___. (Dan. 6:3)
19. And ___ went and returned to Jethro his father in law. (Exod. 4:18)
20. Gaggle of ___.
22. And ___ is the father of Canaan. (Gen. 9:18)
24. British thermal unit (abbr.).
26. ___ -stratus, rainy cloud layer.
28. The labour of the ___ shall fail. (Hab. 3:17)
30. Mimicking cage bird.
32. No man can serve ___ masters. (Matt. 6:24)
33. This wisdom descendeth not from above but is earthly, ___, devilish. (James 3:15)

35. But when ___ heard thereof, he said, It is John whom I beheaded. (Mark 6:16)
37. ___ it therefore in your hearts. (Luke 21:14)
38. The prophet is a ___ of a fowler. (Hos. 9:8)
39. Belonging to the king's chamberlain. (Esther 2:3)
40. And the children of Israel set forward and pitched in ___. (Num. 21:10)

42. Interstitial cell-stimulating hormone substance (abbr.).
45. First garden. (Gen. 2:8)
46. ___ thou doest, do quickly. (John 13:27)
49. Son of Jether. (1 Chron. 7:38)
51. Suffix denoting a tumor.
53. That is.

16

Across

1. Pilate answered, Am I a ___? (John 18:35)
4. Levitical city of Judah. (Josh. 15:42)
9. Eglon was a very ___ man. (Judg. 3:17)
12. All that handle the ___. (Ezek. 27:29)
13. He hath nothing left him in the ___. (Deut. 28:55)
14. Fruit drink.
15. Sin is the ___ of the law. (1 John 3:4)
18. Why is my ___ perpetual? (Jer. 15:18)
19. Titus (abbr.).
20. Plant-eating, nocturnal mammal.
22. Title of Psalm 32.
26. Son of Zerubbabel. (1 Chron. 3:20)
27. Czarist Russian peasant.
28. ___ ye therefore, and teach all nations. (Matt. 28:19)
29. Building the rebellious and the ___ city. (Ezra 4:12)
30. Jewish month. (Neh. 2:1)
31. A city that is ___ on a hill cannot be hid. (Matt. 5:14)
32. Intravenous (abbr.).
33. Lowest point.
34. Son of Uzzi. (1 Chron. 9:8)
35. Of the turkic peoples.
37. All the people that were with him from ___ of Judah. (2 Sam. 6:2)
38. Indianapolis Police Department (abbr.).
39. ___ Magdalene came and told the disciples. (John 20:18)
40. Thy ___ is an everlasting ___. (Ps. 119:142)
46. Expert.
47. To be ambitious (Scot.).
48. Golf gadget.
49. Through.
50. Pains.
51. Equivocate.

Down

1. One ___ or one tittle shall in no wise pass from the law. (Matt. 5:18)
2. Doth not the ___ try words? (Job 12:11)
3. It is ___ up for the slaughter. (Ezek. 21:15)
4. Son of Korah. (Exod. 6:24)
5. An everlasting ___ that shall not be cut off. (Isa. 55:13)
6. Esther put on ___ royal apparel. (Esther 5:1)
7. Or him that stooped for ___. (2 Chron. 36:17)
8. All the fowls of heaven made their ___ [2 words] his boughs. (Ezek. 31:6)
9. By grace are ye saved through ___. (Eph. 2:8)
10. Why make ye this ___ and weep? (Mark 5:39)
11. Were there not ___ cleansed? (Luke 17:17)
16. In that day . . . shall the ___ that is fastened. (Isa. 22:25)
17. Hope deferred maketh the heart ___. (Prov. 13:12)
20. Apocryphal book.
21. I proclaimed a fast there at the river of ___. (Ezra 8:21)
22. Melody.
23. Open.
24. Son of Shemaiah. (1 Chron. 3:22)
25. Ye shall ___ yourselves in your own sight. (Ezek. 20:43)
27. Kind of skirt.
30. Ginseng beverage (2 words).
31. Wrath killeth the foolish man and envy ___ the silly one. (Job 5:2)
33. Naphthalene (abbr.).
34. Merit.
36. Cat breed.
37. The ___ which Solomon had made for the house of the Lord. (2 Kings 25:16)

39. Be ye not as the horse, or as the ___. (Ps. 32:9)

40. Knock.

41. Out of whose womb came the ___? (Job 38:29)

42. Etcetera (abbr.).

43. Old Testament history (abbr.).

44. He maketh the ___ like a pot. (Job 41:31)

45. A time to rend and a time to ___. (Eccles. 3:7)

17

Across

1. They that wait upon the Lord shall ___ their strength. (Isa. 40:31)
6. Now when ___ was come into the province. (Acts 25:1)
12. O come let us ___ Him (from carol).
13. Omen.
14. For though thou wash thee with ___. (Jer. 2:22)
15. Boxer, Muhammad ___.
16. No ___ is of the truth. (1 John 2:21)
17. Science fiction (abbr.).
18. Ancient Scandinavian poet.
20. I will rejoice . . . and ___ out the valley of Succoth. (Ps. 108:7)
21. Go, sell the ___, and pay thy debt. (2 Kings 4:7)
23. Spring.
24. Artist's stand.
25. Blessed are the ___: for they shall inherit the earth. (Matt. 5:5)
27. King of Judah. (2 Kings 15:27)
29. Father of Eliasaph. (Num. 1:14)
31. Canst thou fill his skin with barbed ___? (Job 41:7)
34. Thou shalt plant vineyards and ___ them. (Deut. 28:39)
36. Friend, ___ me three loaves. (Luke 11:5)
38. It hath been declared . . . by them which are of the house of ___. (1 Cor. 1:11)
41. ___ grace of our Lord Jesus Christ . (Rom. 16:24)
43. Tiny.
44. Royal Order Of Soldiers (abbr.).
45. I press toward the mark for the ___. (Phil. 3:14)
47. ___ -Shaddai.
48. American Youth Guard (abbr.).
49. Son of Bela. (1 Chron. 7:7)
50. But he went out . . . to ___ abroad the matter. (Mark 1:45)
52. Native of Scotland.
54. Resource.
55. Delight is not ___ for a fool. (Prov. 19:10)
56. Yet have ___ [2 words] myself servant unto all. (1 Cor. 9:19)

Down

1. To give his life a ___ for many. (Matt. 20:28)
2. But the other is not ___. (1 Cor. 14:17)
3. Is the Lord among us, or ___? (Exod. 17:7)
4. Sins.
5. He reserveth unto us the appointed ___ of harvest. (Jer. 5:24)
6. As a vesture shalt thou ___ them up. (Heb. 1:12)
7. Son of Gad. (Gen. 46:16)
8. John or Luke.
9. TVs.
10. ___ my heart to fear thy name. (Ps. 86:11)
11. Shall iron break the northern iron and the ___? (Jer. 15:12)
13. Primitive (comb. form).
19. Keep me as the ___ of the eye. (Ps. 17:8)
20. Father of Darda (1 Kings 4:31)
22. Shelter.
24. Incline thine ___ unto me. (Ps. 17:6)
26. Fame.
28. Father of Ethan. (1 Chron. 6:44)
30. How long will it be ___ they believe me? (Num. 14:11)
32. Behold all things are become ___. (2 Cor. 5:17)
33. The child ___ seven times. (2 Kings 4:35)
35. ___ you and make you bare. (Isa. 32:11)
37. Erase.

38. Crustaceans with pincers.
39. Rulebook for indoor games.
40. Discourse (comb. form).
42. Father of Naarai. (1 Chron. 11:37)
45. ___ for the peace of Jerusalem. (Ps. 122:6)

46. Extravehicular life support method (abbr.).
49. International Center for Learning (abbr.).
51. Son of Elkanah. (1 Chron 9:16)
53. Electromagnetic (abbr.).

18

Across

1. They discovered a certain creek with a ___. (Acts 27:39)
6. How long shall thy vain thoughts ___ within thee? (Jer. 4:14)
11. Out of Zion, the perfection of beauty, God hath ___. (Ps. 50:2)
12. He esteemeth ___ [2 words] straw. (Job 41:27)
14. We grope as if we ___ no eyes. (Isa. 59:10)
15. Holy Writ.
17. They shall no more ___ it as a proverb in Israel. (Ezek. 12:23)
18. The children of Gad called the altar ___. (Josh. 22:34)
19. And shall be ___ [2 words] breaking forth with blains upon man. (Exod. 9:9)
20. Thanks (Brit.).
21. Their ___ also shall dash the young men to pieces. (Isa. 13:18)
24. Love (Scot.).
25. Son of Zerubbabel. (1 Chron. 3:20)
27. After that ye have suffered ___ [2 words], make you perfect. (1 Peter 5:10)
29. And owls shall dwell there, and ___ shall dance. (Isa. 13:21)
31. ___, ___ lama sabbachthani. (Matt. 27:46)
32. Electric unit.
33. His ___ are his pride, shut up together. (Job 41:15)
36. Daggers.
39. Now, thou son of man . . . wilt thou judge the bloody ___? (Ezek. 22:2)
40. Son of Zephaniah. (Zech. 6:14)
42. Respondez s'il vous plait (please reply).
43. So two ___ three cities wandered unto one city. (Amos 4:8)
44. ___ show (a small display viewed in a box).
46. Moon goddess.

47. Federal Communications Commission (abbr.).
49. And ___ took him Jochebed his father's sister to wife. (Exod. 6:20)
50. Alteration (abbr.).
51. Wringed the dew out of the ___ a bowl full of water. (Judg. 6:38)
53. Belonging to Ethan's father. (1 Chron. 6:44)
55. I have played the fool, and have ___ exceedingly. (1 Sam. 26:21)
56. Covered porticos.

Down

1. I am gone like the ___ when it declineth. (Ps. 109:23)
2. And dig for it more than for ___ treasures. (Job 3:21)
3. Son of Peleth. (Num. 16:1)
4. One of five kings of Midian. (Num. 31:8)
5. Esculent.
6. Consider the ___ of the field, how they grow. (Matt. 6:28)
7. L.A. Dodger pitcher, ___ Hershiser.
8. What have I to ___ with thee? (1 Kings 17:18)
9. Antelope.
10. Intending after ___ to bring him forth to the people. (Acts 12:4)
11. And they had in their inheritance Beersheba, and ___, and Moladah. (Josh. 19:2)
13. I saw when the Lamb opened one of the ___. (Rev. 6:1)
16. Catcall.
22. What is the chaff to the ___? (Jer. 23:28)
23. Ephraim is also like a ___ dove without heart. (Hos. 7:11)
25. For ___ foundation can no man lay. (1 Cor. 3:11)
26. Speaking to yourselves in psalms and ___. (Eph. 5:19)

28. For they prophesy a ___ unto you. (Jer. 27:10)
30. All right.
33. And they shall ___ at the kings. (Hab. 1:10)
34. It is he that sitteth upon the ___ of the earth. (Isa. 40:22)
35. Ye have ___ the counsel of the poor. (Ps. 14:6)
36. Lurks.
37. For ___ [2 words] determined against our master. (1 Sam. 25:17)
38. These are ___ in your feasts of charity. (Jude 12)

41. Why hast thou made us to ___ from thy ways? (Isa. 63:17)
44. The ___ is not to the swift. (Eccles. 9:11)
45. Issue.
48. Wax (comb. form).
50. ___, even the ancient high places are ours. (Ezek. 36:2)
52. She conceived, and bare a son; and he called his name ___. (Gen. 38:3)
54. ___ that they are without excuse. (Rom. 1:20)

19

Across

1. Upon the ___ of the rock. (Job 39:28)
5. And Jacob ___ pottage. (Gen. 25:29)
8. And it ___ worms and stank. (Exod. 16:20)
12. If ye offer the ___ and sick, is it not evil? (Mal. 1:8)
13. ___, I am warm, I have seen the fire. (Isa. 44:16)
14. So must thou bear witness also at ___. (Acts 23:11)
15. Son of Helem. (1 Chron. 7:35)
16. Surname of Thaddaeus. (Matt. 10:3)
18. Buddy.
19. Psalmist's pauses.
20. And they came to ___, where were twelve wells of water. (Exod. 15:27)
22. ___ my soul from their destructions. (Ps. 35:17)
26. His ___ had offended their lord the king of Egypt. (Gen. 40:1)
28. When I had ___ them to the full, they then committed adultery. (Jer. 5:7)
29. Holy Name Society. (abbr.)
30. Climate of Gaza desert.
31. Cheer.
32. Ireland.
33. The heron after her kind, and the lapwing, and the ___. (Deut. 14:18)
34. German (abbr.).
35. Thou beholdest mischief and ___. (Ps. 10:14)
36. One of five golden objects. (1 Sam. 6:4)
38. Platform.
39. Covered carriage.
41. Get thee up into the ___ of Pisgah. (Deut. 3:27)
44. Sugars.
47. He burned the bones of the king of Edom into ___. (Amos 2:1)
48. And drink their own ___ with you? (Isa. 36:12)
49. If any man will ___ thee at the law. (Matt. 5:40)
50. Nobleman.
51. Pier made by thickening a wall.
52. Signed (abbr.).
53. Indigo.

Down

1. All that hear the bruit of thee shall ___ the hands over thee. (Nah. 3:19)
2. In ___ was there a voice heard. (Matt. 2:18)
3. I am an ___. (2 Sam. 1:8)
4. Thicken.
5. For this Melchisedec, king of ___, priest of the most high God. (Heb. 7:1)
6. Son of Zerubbabel. (1 Chron. 3:20)
7. Town of Issachar. (Josh. 21:28)
8. Is my flesh of ___? (Job 6:12)
9. It shall be as the chased ___. (Isa. 13:14)
10. Flightless bird.
11. ___ Moines, Iowa.
17. Bureau of Higher Educational Development (abbr.).
19. ___, I perceive that thou art a prophet. (John 4:19)
21. He hath ___ me and brought me into darkness but not into light. (Lam. 3:2)
23. Almost thou persuadest me to be a ___. (Acts 26:28)
24. One.
25. Anglo-Saxon slave.
26. Ye shall find the ___ wrapped in swaddling clothes. (Luke 2:12)
27. Son of Kemuel. (Gen. 22:21)
28. Be it ___ from me. (1 Sam. 2:30)
31. Who hath ___ of eyes? (Prov. 23:29)

32. Short railroad spur.
34. The ___ had a notable horn. (Dan. 8:5)
35. Israelite judge (abbr.). (1 Sam. 7:15)
37. Father of Joanna. (Luke 3:27)
38. Given medicine.
40. Cozy.

42. Was followed by half the people. (1 Kings 16:21)
43. ___ -mell.
44. Health resort.
45. That I may ___ Christ. (Phil. 3:8)
46. Estimate (abbr.).
47. Meadow.

20

Across

1. He brake the withs, as a thread of ___ is broken. (Judg. 16:9)
4. Though thou shouldest ___ a fool in a mortar. (Prov. 27:22)
8. He ___ on the ground and made clay. (John 9:6)
12. Now a mediator is not a mediator of ___, but God is one. (Gal. 3:20)
13. Even of ___ my people is risen up as an enemy. (Mic. 2:8)
14. Then the king arose and ___ his garments. (2 Sam. 13:31)
15. Seethe ___ for the sons of the prophets. (2 Kings 4:38)
17. Father of Joseph. (Luke 3:30)
18. ___ not liberty for an occasion to the flesh. (Gal. 5:13)
19. Do count them but ___ that I may win Christ. (Phil. 3:8)
20. It is as ___ to a fool to do mischief. (Prov. 10:23)
23. Egypt in the best of the land, the land of ___. (Gen. 47:11)
26. Woe to him that buildeth a ___ with blood. (Hab. 2:12)
27. It is the gall of ___ within him. (Job 20:14)
28. His banner over ___ was love. (Song of Sol. 2:4)
29. His words were softer than ___. (Ps. 55:21)
30. I have led thee in right ___. (Prov. 4:11)
32. For as in Adam all ___. (1 Cor. 15:22)
33. Registered nurse (abbr.).
34. As a ___ is full of birds, so are their houses full of deceit. (Jer. 5:27)
35. The ___ of the fatherless have been broken. (Job 22:9)
36. He became the author of ___ salvation. (Heb. 5:9)
38. Rendezvous.
39. Not with broided ___, or gold, or pearls. (1 Tim. 2:9)
40. Hebrew measure. (2 Kings 6:25)
41. Feat.
43. Province of Asia Minor. (Acts 16:6)
47. Adjutant.
48. Ten women shall ___ your bread in one oven. (Lev. 26:26)
49. Son of Caleb. (1 Chron. 4:15)
50. There followed him a ___ of meat. (2 Sam. 11:8)
51. The ___ of the LORD are upon the righteous. (Ps. 34:15)
52. Nothing.

Down

1. He cropped off the ___ of his young twigs. (Ezek. 17:4)
2. Town of Benjamin. (1 Chron. 8:12)
3. They are ___ with the showers of the mountains. (Job 24:8)
4. With the ___ of thy nostrils the waters were gathered. (Exod. 15:8)
5. Why do the heathen ___ and the people imagine a vain thing? (Ps. 2:1)
6. I took the little book out of the angel's hand and ___ it up. (Rev. 10:10)
7. But ___ are straitened in your own bowels. (2 Cor. 6:12)
8. See what manner of ___ and what buildings are here! (Mark 13:1)
9. ___ and sorrows shall take hold of them. (Isa. 13:8)
10. Son of Jether. (1 Chron. 7:38)
11. ___ acres of vineyard shall yield one bath. (Isa. 5:10)
16. How long will ye ___ my glory into shame? (Ps. 4:2)
17. Vaults.
19. Thou shalt ___ them in pieces like a potter's vessel. (Ps. 2:9)
20. By the same word are kept in ___. (2 Peter 3:7)
21. Yet offend in one ___, he is guilty of all. (James 2:10)

22. I am like an ___ of the desert. (Ps. 102:6)
23. African badger-like animal.
24. Giants. (Deut. 2:10)
25. ___ thou a man that is hasty in his words? (Prov. 29:20)
30. In a ___ [2 words] shall be made with oil. (Lev. 6:21)
31. For this ___ is mount Sinai in Arabia. (Gal. 4:25)
32. O ye ___ bones, hear the word of the LORD (Ezek. 37:4)
34. Chattering birds. (Isa. 38:14)
35. Father of Anak. (Josh. 15:13)
37. Belonging to a certain father. (1 Chron. 8:6)

38. Their words seemed to them as idle ___. (Luke 24:11)
40. Ephraim is a ___ not turned. (Hos. 7:8)
41. Israelite prophet (abbr.). (1 Sam. 3:20)
42. ___ the kine to the cart. (1 Sam. 6:7)
43. Ye have respect to him that weareth the ___ clothing. (James 2:3)
44. All they are brass, and ___ and iron and lead. (Ezek. 22:18)
45. Son of Bela. (1 Chron. 7:7)
46. Take an ___ and thrust it through his ear. (Deut. 15:17)
48. I will see what their end shall ___. (Deut. 32:20)

21

Across

1. They hiss and ___ their head at the daughter of Jerusalem. (Lam. 2:15)
4. But I am carnal, ___ under sin. (Rom. 7:14)
8. It shall not return unto me ___. (Isa. 55:11)
12. But strong meat belongeth to them that are of full ___. (Heb. 5:14)
13. But this man, because he continueth ___. (Heb. 7:24)
14. Yet ___ more I shake not the earth only. (Heb. 12:26)
15. Father of Abner. (1 Sam. 14:51)
16. Son of Ishmael. (Gen. 25:15)
17. Behold, there come two ___ more hereafter. (Rev. 9:12)
18. Your kerchiefs also will I ___. (Ezek. 13:21)
20. I will build again the ___ thereof. (Acts 15:16)
22. Each (abbr.).
24. Whose ___ is destruction, whose God is their belly. (Phil. 3:19)
25. Bachelor of Dramatic Arts (abbr.).
28. California rock bass.
32. Father of Balaam. (Num. 22:5)
33. They ___ through the lusts of the flesh. (2 Peter 2:18)
34. Certain stone heap. (Gen. 31:48)
36. And abundance of peace so long as the ___ endureth. (Ps. 72:7)
37. By his ___ a light doth shine. (Job 41:18)
39. Church bench.
40. Greek letter.
41. He eateth grass as ___ ox. (Job 40:15)
42. I will wipe Jerusalem as a man wipeth ___ [2 words]. (2 Kings 21:13)
44. I did cast them out as the ___ in the streets. (Ps. 18:42)
48. They came and took up his corpse and laid it in a ___. (Mark 6:29)
51. Though ye have ___ among the pots. (Ps. 68:13)
53. The king of ___ in the coast of ___, one. (Josh. 12:23)
54. Ellipse.
55. Saul and the men of Israel . . . pitched by the valley of ___. (1 Sam. 17:2)
56. Divided by strophes.
57. She shall shave her head, and ___ her nails. (Deut. 21:12)
58. And landing at ___ -cuse we tarried there three days. (Acts 28:12)
59. Protection.

Down

1. And he began to be in ___. (Luke 15:14)
2. Askew.
3. Son of Benjamin. (Gen. 46:21)
4. And I will ___ a sign among them. (Isa. 66:19)
5. Hath not the potter power ___ the clay. (Rom. 9:21)
6. O ___, it is not for kings to drink wine. (Prov. 31:4)
7. Depletion.
8. Then all her ___ shall stand. (Num. 30:4)
9. Lod and ___, the valley of crafts-men. (Neh. 11:35)
10. Out of whose womb came the ___? (Job 38:29)
11. ___ Moines, Iowa.
19. Show again.
21. U.S. state (abbr.).
23. The seventh angel poured out his vial into the ___. (Rev. 16:17)
25. A night and a day I have ___ in the deep. (2 Cor. 11:25)
26. Killed eighty-five priests. (1 Sam. 22:18)
27. Belonging to Huppim's brother. (Gen. 46:21)

28. And I will ___ against thee round about. (Isa. 29:3)
29. Maguey.
30. I am consumed by the ___ of thine hand. (Ps. 39:10)
31. Ingredient for Jacob's pottage. (Gen. 25:34)
32. But he that lacketh these things is ___. (2 Peter 1:9)
35. Son of Elkanah. (1 Chron. 9:16)
38. Is not ___ provoked, thinketh no evil. (1 Cor. 13:5)
40. The children of Gad called the altar ___. (Josh. 22:34)
42. No man is ___ to pluck them out of my Father's hand. (John 10:29)

43. This is an hard saying; who can ___ it? (John 6:60)
45. We know that an ___ is nothing in the world. (1 Cor. 8:4)
46. So the posts that ___ upon mules and camels went out. (Esther 8:14)
47. He shall be as an ___ planted by the warm waters. (Jer. 17:8)
48. And there shall be a hole in the ___ of it. (Exod. 28:32)
49. Eggs.
50. After this manner will I ___ the pride of Judah. (Jer. 13:9)
52. National Housing Administration (abbr.).

22

Across

1. And thy estimation shall be of the ___. (Lev. 27:3)
5. Behold, I will cast her into a ___. (Rev. 2:22)
8. It is a present ___ unto my lord Esau. (Gen. 32:18)
12. Bringing gold, and silver, ivory and ___, and peacocks. (1 Kings 10:22)
13. For Adam was first formed, then ___. (1 Tim. 2:13)
14. For lo, the winter is past, the rain is ___ and gone. (Song of Sol. 2:11)
15. Hatred (comb. form).
16. Being reviled, we ___; being persecuted, we suffer it. (1 Cor. 4:12)
18. Son of Gad. (Gen. 46:16)
19. Because they ___ not the children of Israel with bread. (Neh. 13:2)
20. Our belly cleaveth unto the ___. (Ps. 44:25)
21. Royal Geographical Society (abbr.).
22. Officer Candidate (abbr.).
23. And there are three that bear witness ___ earth. (1 John 5:8)
24. They set a ___, they catch men. (Jer. 5:26)
26. That ___ the name of Jesus every knee should bow. (Phil. 2:10)
27. The mouth of the foolish is ___ destruction. (Prov. 10:14)
29. When I lift up my hands toward thy holy ___. (Ps. 28:2)
31. Behold, there come two ___ more hereafter. (Rev. 9:12)
34. ___ [2 words] remnant of them shall return. (Isa. 10:22)
35. I should have slept: then had I ___ [2 words] rest. (Job 3:13)
37. When they had sung an ___ they went out. (Mark 14:26)
40. Son of Peleth. (Num. 16:1)
41. There shall come a ___ out of Jacob. (Num. 24:17)
43. Thou shalt love thy neighbour ___ thyself. (Matt. 19:19)
44. Art thou better than populous ___. (Nah. 3:8)
45. There shall come forth a ___ out of the stem of Jesse. (Isa. 11:1)
47. The Ezrahite. (1 Kings 4:31)
49. Asian peoples.
50. Pair.
51. Uproars.
52. Doth the wild ___ bray when he hath grass? (Job 6:5)
53. As one gathereth ___ that are left. (Isa. 10:14)
55. Poem.
56. Perfume source. (Prov. 7:17)
57. Flightless bird.
58. Nicotinamide-adenine dinucleotide (abbr.).
59. Wrought iron and brass to ___ the house. (2 Chron. 24:12)

Down

1. Make to yourselves friends of the ___ of unrighteousness. (Luke 16:9)
2. Neither have two coats ___. (Luke 9:3)
3. Watch and pray ___ ye enter into temptation. (Mark 14:38)
4. Einsteinium (sym.).
5. Son of Beor. (Gen. 36:32)
6. Overthrow.
7. For the Son of man is not come to ___ men's lives. (Luke 9:56)
8. King of Egypt. (2 Kings 17:4)
9. For Hiram was ___ a lover of David. (1 Kings 5:1)
10. The men of Cuth made ___, and the men of Hamath made Ashima. (2 Kings 17:30)
11. Sad.
16. With Zechariah and Jaaziel. (1 Chron. 15:18)

17. Israelites went down to the Philistines, to sharpen any man his ___. (1 Sam. 13:20)
23. Canst thou fill his skin with barbed ___? (Job 41:7)
25. And make straight ___ for your feet. (Heb. 12:13)
28. My heart standeth in ___ of thy word. (Ps. 119:161)
30. Coral reef.
32. Out of the ___ came forth meat. (Judg. 14:14)
33. And I will drive thee from thy ___. (Isa. 22:19)
35. And Hamath also shall ___ thereby. (Zech. 9:2)

36. He that followeth after vain persons shall have poverty ___. (Prov. 28:19)
38. Old disciple of Cyprus. (Acts 21:16)
39. Spoke loudly.
42. Forgot to let Peter in. (Acts 12:13, 14)
43. Answer (abbr.).
46. Chief magistrate of Venice.
48. Adjective (suffix).
49. That they should bring them in and out by ___. (1 Chron. 9:28)
54. Salvation Army (abbr.).
56. I ___ that I ___. (Exod. 3:14)

49

23

Across

1. What vehement desire, yea what zeal, yea, what ___! (2 Cor. 7:11)
8. There ___ no small stir about that way. (Acts 19:23)
13. City of Judah. (2 Chron. 11:9)
14. The eleventh month. (Zech. 1:7)
15. A time to rend, and a time to ___. (Eccles. 3:7)
16. Recede.
17. I will come by you into ___. (Rom. 15:28)
18. Irish Gaelic.
20. And will set them to ___ his ground and to reap. (1 Sam. 8:12)
22. Widemouthed earthenware pot.
23. And ___, the heavens were opened unto him. (Matt. 3:16)
25. A poor man is better than a ___. (Prov. 19:22)
27. The way of the righteous is made ___. (Prov. 15:19)
30. Let now . . . the ___ prognosticators stand up. (Isa. 47:13)
34. Iodine (comb. form).
35. ___ there be therefore any consolation in Christ. (Phil. 2:1)
37. Him therefore I hope ___ send presently. (Phil. 2:23)
38. Open (archaic).
39. Ye make him ___ more the child of hell. (Matt. 23:15)
42. The great goddess ___ should be despised. (Acts 19:27)
44. Confederate of Abram. (Gen. 14:13)
45. Altar erected by several tribes. (Josh. 22:34)
46. The wall fell down ___. (Josh. 6:20)
49. District of Palestine. (Josh. 11:2)
51. Father of Gaal. (Judg. 9:26)
55. Thy bow was made quite naked according to the ___. (Hab. 3:9)
57. Parti-colored animal.
59. Canticle.
60. All thy garments smell of myrrh, and ___. (Ps. 45:8)
61. Be not carried about with divers and ___ doctrines. (Heb. 13:9)
63. Unto ___, unto the city of Arbah. (Gen. 35:27)
64. For her bowels ___ upon her son. (1 Kings 3:26)

Down

1. ___ it, ___ it, even to the foundation thereof. (Ps. 137:7)
2. City of Judah. (Josh. 15:21)
3. This day have I payed my ___. (Prov. 7:14)
4. Father of Elmodam. (Luke 3:28)
5. None (Scot.).
6. Scoff.
7. Joseph commanded his servants . . . to ___ his father. (Gen. 50:2)
8. The dumb ___ speaking with man's voice. (2 Peter 2:16)
9. For by it the elders obtained a good ___. (Heb. 11:2)
10. Son of Joktan. (Gen. 10:28)
11. Fine linen . . . which thou spreadest forth to be thy ___. (Ezek. 27:7)
12. Volcano in Sicily.
19. Now the sons of ___ were sons of Belial. (1 Sam. 2:12)
21. As they that count it pleasure to ___ in the day time. (2 Peter 2:13)
24. Pungent bulb. (Num. 11:5)
26. Negative terminal of a storage battery delivering current.
27. The mouth of strange women is a deep ___. (Prov. 22:14)
28. Let the brother of ___ degree rejoice. (James 1:9)
29. Why make ye this ___, and weep? (Mark 5:39)
31. A call to excite attention.
32. Licensed practical nurse (abbr.).
33. For all the promises of God in him are ___. (2 Cor. 1:20)

36. For the men knew that he ___ from the presence of the Lord. (Jonah 1:10)
40. As my ___ hath sent me, even so send I you. (John 20:21)
41. There was a certain man before him which had the ___. (Luke 14:2)
43. Chemical compound (suff.).
46. Her king is cut off as the ___ upon the water. (Hos. 10:7)
47. Ooh ___ ___!
48. ___ bomb.

50. Ye shall keep it in appointed season: according to all the ___ (sing.) of it. (Num. 9:3)
52. West German capital.
53. If the iron be blunt and he do not whet the ___. (Eccles. 10:10)
54. And whatsoever ye do in word or ___. (Col. 3:17)
56. Compass point.
58. Epoch.
62. Argon (symbol).

24

Across

1. ___ strangers shall fade away. (Ps. 18:45)
4. For every head shall be ___. (Jer. 48:37)
8. Because the love of God is ___ abroad in our hearts. (Rom. 5:5)
12. His words were softer than ___. (Ps. 55:21)
13. Of the tribe of ___ were sealed twelve thousand. (Rev. 7:6)
14. ___ is the patience and the faith of the saints. (Rev. 13:10)
15. Son of Bela. (1 Chron. 7:7)
16. And they arrived at the country of the ___. (Luke 8:26)
18. French article.
19. We have four men which have a ___ on them. (Acts 21:23)
20. The children of ___. (Ezra 2:57)
23. The Babylonians came to her into the ___ of love. (Ezek. 23:17)
24. Coffee cup.
27. A certain disciple ___ . . . this woman was full of good works and almsdeeds. (Acts 9:36)
30. Oldest son of Caleb. (1 Chron. 4:15)
31. Prophet of the Lord. (2 Chron. 28:9)
32. It shall ___ thee up like the cankerworm. (Nah. 3:15)
34. Learn to maintain good works for necessary ___. (Titus 3:14).
35. Pauline epistle (abbr.).
36. Blessed be the Lord who daily ___ us with benefits. (Ps. 68:19)
38. Variation of edh.
39. Son of Shamer. (1 Chron. 7:34)
41. High craggy hill.
42. ___ no man any thing, but to love one another. (Rom. 13:8)
43. ___, our eye hath seen it. (Ps. 35:21)
46. I will speak that I may be ___. (Job 32:20)

52. Let them shut the doors and ___ them. (Neh. 7:3)
53. Within as it were an half ___ of land. (1 Sam. 14:14)
54. My couch shall ___ my complaint. (Job 7:13)
55. Men of high degree are a ___. (Ps. 62:9)
56. ___ was over all the host of Israel. (2 Sam. 20:23)
57. Exceeding in ___ attire upon their heads. (Ezek. 23:15)
58. Epoch.

Down

1. They ___ not, neither do they spin. (Matt. 6:28)
2. For the labourer is worthy of his ___. (Luke 10:7)
3. Zacharias's wife. (Luke 1:5)
4. For some of them thought, because Judas had the ___. (John 13:29)
5. Father of Berechiah. (1 Chron. 9:16)
6. They thirsted not when he ___ them through the deserts. (Isa. 48:21)
7. And he ___ them from the judgment seat. (Acts 18:16)
8. But I shall ___ you plainly of the Father. (John 16:25)
9. Son of Zephaniah. (Zech. 6:14)
10. How long will it be ___ they attain to innocency? (Hos. 8:5)
11. ___ Plaines, Illinois.
17. Thy ___ and thy staff they comfort me. (Ps. 23:4)
21. Central.
22. Pardon my iniquity; for ___ is great. (Ps. 25:11)
23. And shalt call me no more ___. (Hos. 2:16)
24. ___ comforters are ye all. (Job 16:2)
25. Suffix same as -ide.
26. And our eyelids ___ out with waters. (Jer. 9:18)

52

27. Carry.
28. Entrance.
29. The LORD reigneth; ___ is clothed with majesty. (Ps. 93:1)
33. But I trust ___ come unto you and speak face to face. (2 John 12)
34. Bushy Japanese plant.
37. That ___ the name of Jesus every knee should bow. (Phil. 2:10)
39. Let all the inhabitants of the world stand in ___ of him. (Ps. 33:8)
40. Father of Elon-beth-hanan. (1 Kings 4:9, 10)

42. Two princes of the Midianites ___ and Zeeb. (Judg. 7:25)
44. Cut off thine ___. (Jer. 7:29)
45. Region.
46. Reign (Hindu).
47. Environment (comb. form).
48. Brother.
49. For the ___ is withered away. (Isa. 15:6)
50. Compass point.
51. Dedication (abbr.).

25

Across

1. Ye shall ___ yourselves in your own sight. (Ezek. 20:43)
6. Through his ___ also he shall cause craft to prosper. (Dan. 8:25)
12. Son of Joktan. (Gen. 10:29)
13. Son of Azareel. (Neh. 11:13)
15. Girl's name.
16. Foliage stem.
17. Wildebeest.
18. Let his children be continually vagabonds and ___. (Ps. 109:10)
19. Wooden runner.
20. Uncover thy locks, make bare the ___. (Isa. 47:2)
21. Daughter of Asher. (Gen. 46:17)
23. Compass point.
24. Son of Dishon. (Gen. 36:26)
26. ___ of Galilee.
28. Father of Nathan. (1 Chron. 2:36)
29. And the plague ___ in upon them. (Ps. 106:29)
33. Deoxyribonucleic acid.
35. To ___ with the fine flour. (Ezek. 46:14)
36. An ephah for a ___. (Ezek. 45:24)
39. River flowing through Rome.
41. Valuable mineral.
42. Evangelical Bible Associated Churches (abbr.).
44. The highways ___ waste. (Isa. 33:8)
45. Labor National Congress (abbr.).
46. Jason's sailors (2 words).
48. Divide.
50. Having udders.
51. Overact.
52. Mary's sister. (John 11:1)
53. For I mean not that other men be ___. (2 Cor. 8:13)

Down

1. Lengthy pasture (2 words).
2. Thou ___ thine hand, they are filled with good. (Ps. 104:28)
3. Bringing into captivity every ___. (2 Cor. 10:5)
4. ___ only shalt thou serve. (Matt. 4:10)
5. Time.
6. I would not write with ___ and ink. (2 John 12)
7. Particular Greek letters.
8. Language of the Vulgate Bible (abbr.).
9. Wife of Osiris.
10. And the deceitfulness of riches ___ the word. (Matt. 13:22)
11. Belonging to a particular Ivy League school.
14. Institute of Electrical and Electronic Engineers (abbr.).
18. Certain Levite. (1 Chron. 15:18)
21. Salute every ___ in Christ Jesus. (Phil. 4:21)
22. Son of Beriah. (Gen. 46:17)
25. Which could not be eaten, they were so ___. (Jer. 24:2)
27. He shall gather the lambs with his ___. (Isa. 40:11)
30. An eloquent man, mighty in the scriptures. (Acts 18:24)
31. Source of borax.
32. And he ___ there an altar. (Gen. 33:20)
34. What ___ thee now? (Isa. 22:1)
35. Golf gadget.
36. Quantity of paper.
37. Son of Terah. (Gen. 11:26)
38. Molten rock.
40. Son of Moza. (1 Chron. 8:37)
43. Commissioner (abbr.).
47. Matthew (abbr.).
48. And the LORD came down to ___ the city. (Gen. 11:5)
49. Prime Minister's Attache (abbr.).

26

Across

1. I will cut off the ___ of the idols. (Zech. 13:2)
6. The love of God is ___ abroad in our hearts. (Rom. 5:5)
10. ___ ye thither unto us: our God shall fight for us. (Neh. 4:20)
11. Tack.
14. Minor prophet.
15. African country.
16. Baseball statistic (abbr.).
17. And David . . . took thence a stone and ___ it. (1 Sam. 17:49)
19. ___ -dik, African antelope.
20. Slave.
22. But Jehoiada . . . bored a hole in the ___ of it. (2 Kings 12:9)
23. And the devil . . . was cast into the ___ of fire. (Rev. 20:10)
24. Son of Caleb. (1 Chron. 2:18)
26. Reigned in Jehoshaphat's stead. (1 Kings 22:50)
28. The Berothite (1 Chron. 11:39)
30. Prince of Issachar (Num. 34:26).
33. Behaiah . . . slew a lion in a pit in a ___ day. (1 Chron. 11:22)
37. Son of Seth (Gen. 4:26).
38. Iodine (comb. form).
40. Over Edom will I cast out my ___. (Ps. 60:8)
41. So he smote him therewith in the fifth ___. (2 Sam. 20:10)
42. The lamb as a Christian emblem.
44. Master of Library Science (abbr.).
45. Major prophet.
47. Cover with concrete again.
49. He ___ [2 words] the vineyard unto keepers. (Song of Sol. 8:11)
50. Military blockades.
51. Austrian river.
52. I see men as ___, walking. (Mark 8:24)

Down

1. Howbeit there is a kinsman ___than I. (Ruth 3:12)
2. Home of the Norse gods.
3. Move away.
4. Epochs.
5. If they abide not ___ in unbelief, shall be graffed in. (Rom. 11:23)
6. For I have heard the ___ of many. (Ps. 31:13)
7. Wherefore lift up the hands which ___ down. (Heb. 12:12)
8. Evening (abbr.).
9. East Indian cedar.
10. Ancestor of Jesus. (Luke 3:27)
12. ___ the Harodite. (2 Sam. 23:25)
13. Brother of Ulam. (1 Chron. 7:16)
18. City of Dan. (Josh. 21:24)
21. Baptismal water receptacles.
23. Wherefore gird up the ___ of your mind. (1 Peter 1:13)
25. North American Indian (abbr.).
27. Hath.
29. I will ascend above the ___ of the clouds. (Isa. 14:14)
30. We gat our bread with the ___ of our lives. (Lam. 5:9)
31. Ye pay tithe of mint and ___ and cummin. (Matt. 23:23)
32. Having lobes.
34. Level of resistance of a conductor.
35. Their horses . . . are more fierce than the evening ___. (Hab. 1:8)
36. Affirmative votes.
39. Then Moses trembled, and ___ not behold. (Acts 7:32)
42. American Association for the United Nations (abbr.).
43. Along the route from Horeb to Kadesh-barnea. (Deut. 1:2)
46. Atom.
48. Letter of the alphabet.

27

Across

1. Authored Psalm 89.
6. Jacob was wroth and ___ with Laban. (Gen. 31:36)
11. Wound for wound, ___ for ___. (Exod. 21:25)
12. Calcium carbonate rock.
14. ___ it turneth, it prospereth. (Prov. 17:8)
16. Of the alimentary canal.
17. Composition for two.
18. Do they not ___ that devise evil? (Prov. 14:22)
19. River in Thailand.
20. Yet will I not ___ thee. (Matt. 26:35)
21. White-tailed sea eagle.
22. Most recent.
24. Though I forbear, what am I ___? (Job 16:6)
25. Happy is the man that ___ [2 words] quiver full. (Ps. 127:5)
27. She painted her face, and ___ her head. (2 Kings 9:30)
30. We have borne the image of the ___. (1 Cor. 15:49)
33. Father of Ahira. (Num. 1:15)
34. Ox (Scot.).
35. Order of the Eastern Star (abbr.).
37. No commercial value (abbr.).
38. Academy (abbr.).
39. Allied Military Legion Excursion (abbr.).
40. Parched bird from Baltimore [2 words].
43. Greek goddess of the hearth.
44. Point at the root of the nose.
45. Son of Bani. (Ezra 10:29)
46. He shall surely ___ her to be his wife. (Exod. 22:16)

Down

1. Son of Helah. (1 Chron. 4:7)
2. Characteristic of the Godhead.
3. Blows.
4. Prefix meaning away.
5. And ___ not that any man should ask thee. (John 16:30)
6. Contented.
7. Owl cry.
8. Spanish cheer.
9. Thou shalt not sow thy vineyard with ___ seeds. (Deut. 22:9)
10. Infinite (archaic).
11. Unclean bird. (Deut. 14:16)
13. I have played the fool and have ___ exceedingly. (1 Sam. 26:21)
15. I will ___ [3 words] of thy commandments. (Ps. 119:32)
20. For he that is ___ is freed from sin. (Rom. 6:7)
21. As the lightning cometh out of the ___. (Matt. 24:27)
23. ___ he shall appear, we may have confidence. (1 John 2:28)
24. Ireland.
26. Completed (2 words).
27. But yet in it shall be a ___. (Isa. 6:13)
28. Baseball is a game of ___.
29. Plunder.
31. Similar (comb. form).
32. The priest shall not seek for ___ hair. (Lev. 13:36)
34. Number system with a base of eight.
36. The evidence of things not ___. (Heb. 11:1)
38. Whom all ___ and the world worshippeth. (Acts 19:27)
39. Agricultural Institute of South Dakota (abbr.).
41. Route (abbr.).
42. ___ greedily after the error of Balaam. (Jude 11)

28

Across

1. Puzzling question.
6. I found Israel like ___ in the wilderness. (Hos. 9:10)
12. Syrian ruler. (2 Cor. 11:32)
14. ___ ye: for the kingdom of heaven is at hand. (Matt. 3:2)
15. Clog shoe.
16. Restaurant.
17. Atomic tellurium (abbr.).
18. Balak the king of Moab hath brought me from ___. (Num. 23:7)
20. Accomplice.
21. ___ to her that is filthy. (Zeph. 3:1)
22. Thou shalt burn it in the fire; it is ___ inward. (Lev. 13:55)
23. Kind of lily.
24. The disciples . . . determined to send ___ unto the brethren. (Acts 11:29)
26. Tarry.
27. Let him seek peace and ___ [2 words]. (1 Peter 3:11)
29. And he shall ___ the sheaf before the Lord. (Lev. 23:11)
31. Flashily attractive.
34. But what are they among so ___? (John 6:9)
35. They made upon the ___ of the robe pomegranates. (Exod. 39:24)
36. Son of Bani. (Ezra 10:34)
38. Greek letter.
39. Foretell.
40. Hillside.
41. Massive tropical trees.
43. None of them was cleansed, saving Naaman the ___. (Luke 4:27)
45. Bassinet.
46. But ___ [2 words] is bitter as wormwood. (Prov. 5:4)
47. Idol made by the men of Hamath. (2 Kings 17:30)
48. Unites.

Down

1. Fruit.
2. With a certain ___ who informed the governor against Paul. (Acts 24:1)
3. Sofa.
4. Little one (suff.).
5. John ___, Scottish arctic explorer.
6. Be exceeding glad: for ___ is your reward in heaven. (Matt. 5:12)
7. Quantity of paper.
8. Given to hospitality, ___ to teach. (1 Tim. 3:2)
9. There was none that moved the wing . . . or ___. (Isa. 10:14)
10. Infuriate.
11. Pillar (comb. form).
13. Thorns and ___ are in the way of the froward. (Prov. 22:5)
19. But they have ___ to receive correction. (Jer. 5:3)
22. Make ready quickly three measures of ___ meal. (Gen. 18:6)
23. Therapeutic bath.
25. Upon those did Solomon ___ a tribute of bondservice. (1 Kings 9:21)
26. Leaning.
28. Catch.
29. Let the ___ under the heaven be gathered. (Gen. 1:9)
30. Stood beside Ezra. (Neh. 8:4)
32. Son of Abihail. (Num. 3:35)
33. Our word toward you was not ___ [2 words] nay. (2 Cor. 1:18)
34. Holy city of Islam.
35. Minor prophet.
37. Furnishes.
39. Is there no ___ in Gilead? (Jer. 8:22)
40. Bromine and rhenium symbols.
42. Bank discount interest (abbr.).
44. Eurasian evergreen.

29

Across

1. One of Noah's sons. (Gen. 7:13)
4. Lest at any time we should let them ___. (Heb. 2:1)
8. I will shoot three arrows on the ___ thereof. (1 Sam. 20:20)
12. Eggs.
13. His violent dealing shall come down upon his own ___. (Ps. 7:16)
14. Where John was baptizing (alternate spelling). (John 3:23)
15. Thou girdest thyself and ___ whither thou wouldest. (John 21:18)
17. And they came to the threshingfloor of ___. (Gen. 50:10).
18. Hostels.
19. Be still ye inhabitants of the ___. (Isa. 23:2)
21. Tax.
22. To whom hast thou ___ words? (Job 26:4)
25. And entering into a ___ of Adramyttium, we launched. (Acts 27:2)
26. When he hath ___ [3 words] shall come forth as gold. (Job 23:10)
27. Office of Economic Opportunity (abbr.).
28. Gas used in electric tubes.
29. How long will it be ___ they attain to innocency? (Hos. 8:5)
30. I served thee ___ years for thy two daughters. (Gen. 31:41)
32. Revise.
33. Synonymous with too [2 words].
34. So also shall the rich man ___ away in his ways. (James 1:11)
35. Girl's name.
36. Wrap.
37. Before your pots can ___ the thorns. (Ps. 58:9)
39. And eateth not the bread of ___. (Prov. 31:27)
43. Ah, I will ___ me of mine adversaries. (Isa. 1:24)
44. Loyal (Scottish).
45. Oolong or Pekoe.
46. Department of Research and Scientific Development (abbr.).
47. Plants.
48. Wood, ___, stubble. (1 Cor. 3:12)

Down

1. Take heed therefore ___ ye hear. (Luke 8:18)
2. And the king of Assyria brought men from . . . ___. (2 Kings 17:24)
3. Not using your liberty for a cloke of ___. (1 Peter 2:16)
4. For my life is ___ with grief. (Ps. 31:10)
5. The Angel which redeemed me . bless the ___. (Gen. 48:16)
6. That which groweth of ___ own accord of thy harvest. (Lev. 25:5)
7. Let my life be given me at my ___. (Esther 7:3)
8. My transgression is ___ up in a bag. (Job. 14:17).
9. Seeketh and ___ with all wisdom. (Prov. 18:1)
10. Dead on arrival (abbr.).
11. For the ___ of those things is death. (Rom. 6:21)
16. With a ___ and a flower in one branch. (Exod. 25:33)
20. British machine carbine.
21. Hebrew place of the dead.
22. And he ___ him and he took it. (Gen. 33:11)
23. Weird.
24. There was a continual ___ given him of the king. (Jer. 52:34)
25. Davenport.
26. Shipbuilding pegs.
28. Until the days of your consecration be ___ [2 words] end. (Lev. 8:33)
31. Disturbed.
32. Merit.
34. Wood and coal.
36. Defect.

37. I have ___ you with milk. (1 Cor. 3:2)
38. He that planted the ___, shall he not hear? (Ps. 94:9)
40. ___ Gratias (Latin)—thanks to God.
41. And the ___ was set above upon them. (1 Kings 7:25)
42. But whom ___ ye that I am? (Matt. 16:15)

30

Across

1. We ___ by the flesh pots. (Exod. 16:3)
4. Son of Simeon. (Gen. 46:10)
8. Son of Shem. (Gen. 10:22)
12. Thought Hannah was drunk. (1 Sam. 1:14)
13. Whosoever shall say to his brother, ___, shall be in danger. (Matt. 5:22)
14. King of Sodom. (Gen. 14:2)
15. He was despised and we ___ him not. (Isa. 53:3)
17. And the border . . . round about shall be a ___. (Ezek. 43:13)
18. Even a child is known by his ___. (Prov. 20:11)
19. Margarine.
21. A sword is upon the liars; and they shall ___. (Jer. 50:36)
23. Concerning [2 words].
25. But I have ___ and abound: I am full. (Phil. 4:18)
28. Their widows were ___ in the daily ministration. (Acts 6:1)
31. Their widows are increased to me above the sand of the ___. (Jer. 15:8)
33. Not with Adonijah. (1 Kings 1:8)
34. Elusive.
35. They have now ___ us in our steps. (Ps. 17:11)
38. Distinguished Service Order (abbr.).
39. Light.
40. Ye shall find an ass ___, and a colt with her. (Matt. 21:2)
42. I went down into the garden of ___ to see the fruits. (Song of Sol. 6:11)
44. Shade.
48. Let down your ___ for a draught. (Luke 5:4)
50. And not only idle, but ___ also and busybodies. (1 Tim. 5:13)
52. That the word of the Lord may have ___ course. (2 Thess. 3:1)
53. Throb.
54. Punch.
55. Covers.
56. Where Jotham fled. (Judg. 9:21)
57. Who came in privily to ___ out our liberty. (Gal. 2:4)

Down

1. So the holy ___ shall be the substance thereof. (Isa. 6:13)
2. But will ye weary my God ___? (Isa. 7:13)
3. South American monkey.
4. ___ Trail.
5. Rodents.
6. Expert.
7. Set into a groove.
8. But now much more in my ___. (Phil, 2:12)
9. This saying is commonly ___ among the Jews. (Matt. 28:15)
10. Son of Jether. (1 Chron. 7:38)
11. Shall a ___ be more pure than his maker? (Job 4:17)
16. For Christ is the ___ of the law for righteousness. (Rom. 10:4)
20. Should I ___ against my right? (Job 34:6)
22. Defecate.
24. Lampreys.
25. Ascus (comb. form).
26. Gospel musician, ___ Patillo.
27. We have mourned unto you, and ye have not ___. (Matt. 11:17)
29. Like the slain that ___ [3 words] grave. (Ps. 88:5)
30. Two (comb. form).
32. And your ___ shall commit adultery. (Hos. 4:13)
36. Go to the ___ thou sluggard. (Prov. 6:6)
37. Secondary (comb. form).
41. ___ Segno, repeat sign in music.
43. Knife.
45. Beaks.

46. I will ___ off from the top of his young twigs. (Ezek. 17:22)
47. O inhabitant of Aroer, stand by the way and ___. (Jer. 48:19)
48. Sports league.
49. Son of Gad. (Gen. 46:16)
51. Hero.

31

Across

1. I will requite thee in this ___, saith the LORD (2 Kings 9:26)
5. ___ to righteousness and sin not. (1 Cor. 15:34)
10. They ___ the persons of men and vessels of brass. (Ezek. 27:13)
12. When a man shall have in the skin of his flesh a ___. (Lev. 13:2)
14. Son of man, put forth a ___. (Ezek. 17:2)
15. A Moabite. (1 Chron. 11:46)
16. He casteth forth his ___ like morsels. (Ps. 147:17)
17. Hebrew measure of weight. (Ezek. 45:12)
19. Suffix denoting tumor.
20. The LORD God of the Hebrews hath ___ with us. (Exod. 3:18)
21. Jewish month. (Neh. 6:15)
22. Son of Seth. (Gen. 4:26)
23. A city of Shechem. (Gen. 33:18)
25. On the left side.
26. Belonging to a certain gate. (1 Chron. 26:18)
28. Unto the plain of ___. (Gen. 12:6)
31. The king's decree . . . shall be published throughout all his ___. (Esther 1:20)
34. I have commanded my sanctified ___. (Isa. 13:3)
35. Son of Ulla. (1 Chron. 7:39)
36. Unit of work.
38. New York State (abbr.).
39. Son of Ishmael. (1 Chron. 1:30)
40. Compass point.
41. Father of Baal-hanan. (Gen. 36:39)
43. Perennial crownvetch.
45. Japanese religion.
46. ___ [3 words], and there is none like me. (Isa. 46:9)
47. Cook's covering.
48. Render therefore to all their ___. (Rom. 13:7)

Down

1. And brought the ___ of the things that were sold. (Acts 4:34)
2. And to him that ___ himself with thick clay! (Hab. 2:6)
3. And beside this, giving all diligence, ___ to your faith. (2 Peter 1:5)
4. A place in Babylonia. (Ezra 2:59)
5. Symbolic name for Jerusalem. (Isa. 29:1)
6. Thou shalt break them ___ a rod of iron. (Ps. 2:9)
7. He planteth an ___, and the rain doth nourish it. (Isa. 44:14)
8. Dressing gown.
9. Captivate.
10. Clip.
11. The treacherous ___ dealeth treacherously. (Isa. 21:2)
13. Terrified.
18. Authored by Moses.
22. ___ -lon, Greek letter.
24. Animal cargo for Solomon. (1 Kings 10:22)
25. Son of Shem. (Gen. 10:22)
27. Priest and trumpeter. (1 Chron. 15:24)
28. Indestructible unit.
29. Sweet spice. (Exod. 30:34)
30. Transfer to another vessel.
32. Finagle.
33. Sea eagle bone (2 words).
35. (Elisabeth) was of the daughters of ___. (Luke 1:5)
37. A pike fish (Scot.).
39. ___, all-terrain bike race.
42. Bank note received (abbr.).
44. Southern Methodist University (abbr.).

32

Across

1. Paul and Barnabas split up over him. (Acts 15:39)
5. And dust shall be the serpent's ___. (Isa. 65:25)
9. The children of ___. (Ezra 2:57)
11. Come now, and let us ___ together. (Isa. 1:18)
13. Member of Jewish sect.
14. Go to the ___ thou sluggard. (Prov. 6:6)
15. But ___ are not of them who draw back unto perdition. (Heb. 10:39)
16. Until the day that ___ entered into the ark. (Matt. 24:38)
17. Prolific psalmist.
19. Wilt thou ___ thine eyes on that which is not? (Prov. 23:5)
20. From Hebron, from Debir, from ___. (Josh. 11:21)
22. ___ his son, Jehoshuah his son. (1 Chron. 7:27)
23. ___ what must I do to be saved? (Acts 16:30)
24. Blinded by God. (Acts 9:8).
26. Values.
28. That the ___ of men might seek after the Lord. (Acts 15:17)
30. And the king sealed it with his own ___. (Dan. 6:17)
32. As the partridge sitteth on ___ and hatcheth them not. (Jer. 17:11)
35. Then Paul stood in the midst of ___ hill. (Acts 17:22)
36. He was ___ as a sheep to the slaughter. (Acts 8:32)
38. Righteousness and peace have kissed ___ other. (Ps. 85:10)
40. Father of Bezaleel. (Exod. 31:2)
41. Rebuke not an ___, but intreat him as a father. (1 Tim. 5:1)
43. Pull (Scot.).
44. Audiophile's new medium (abbr.).
45. Fruit drink.
46. Belonging to Simeon. (Acts 13:1)
48. So are my ways ___ than your ways. (Isa. 55:9)
50. And with these sayings ___ restrained they the people. (Acts 14:18)
51. Rise.
52. Mixture.

Down

1. And he set ___ to hew wrought stones. (1 Chron. 22:2)
2. For the king had ___ [3 words] navy of Tharshish. (1 Kings 10:22)
3. Route (abbr.).
4. And be ye ___ one to another, tenderhearted. (Eph. 4:32)
5. Wrought iron and brass to ___ the house of the LORD (2 Chron. 24:12)
6. Open thy mouth, and ___ that I give thee. (Ezek. 2:8)
7. ___ the hart panteth after the water brooks. (Ps. 42:1)
8. Also he built ___ in the desert. (2 Chron. 26:10)
9. Where are the gods of Sepharvaim, ___, and Ivah? (2 Kings 18:34)
10. Yet will they ___ upon the LORD. (Mic. 3:11)
11. It ___ fire and brimstone from heaven. (Luke 17:29)
12. ___ of checker work, and wreaths of chain work. (1 Kings 7:17)
18. And it ___ out Jonah upon the day land. (Jonah 2:10)
19. I will ___ also upon the mount of the congregation. (Isa. 14:13)
21. Towns.
23. He hath laid ___ against us. (Mic. 5:1)
25. Leonard (abbr.).
27. For ye tithe mint and ___ and all manner of herbs. (Luke 11:42)
29. Lydia, a ___ of purple. (Acts 16:14)
30. One of the seven churches in Asia. (Rev. 1:11)

Across / Down Clues

31. Son of Bela. (1 Chron. 7:7)
33. Large sluggish burrowing clams.
34. And power was given unto him to ___ men with fire. (Rev. 16:8)
35. And so ___ the more as ye see the day approaching. (Heb. 10:25)
37. They wandered in deserts, and in mountains, and in ___. (Heb. 11:38)
39. Stockings.
41. Toward the cost of Edom southward were Kabzeel and ___. (Josh. 15:21)

42. Go to now, ye ___ men, weep and howl. (James 5:1)
45. ___, even the ancient high places are ours. (Ezek. 36:2)
47. German anti-aircraft (abbr.).
49. I ___ to prepare a place for you. (John 14:2)

33

Across

1. Behold the fowls of the air; for they ___ not. (Matt. 6:26)
4. The wilderness hath ___ them in. (Exod. 14:3)
8. Hypocrisy.
12. But the glory of the celestial is ___. (1 Cor. 15:40)
13. Deliver me out of the ___. (Ps. 69:14)
14. The sucking child shall play on the ___ of the asp. (Isa. 11:8)
15. John ___ Passos, American author.
16. ___ and Thummim. (Neh. 7:65)
17. Judged Israel ten years. (Judg. 12:11)
18. ___ -a-tete.
20. And at midnight Paul and Silas ___. (Acts 16:25)
22. So now [2 words] not you that sent me hither. (Gen. 45:8)
24. Their visage is blacker than a ___. (Lam. 4:8)
25. Which make a noise like the noise of the ___. (Isa. 17:12)
26. Hold fast the ___ of sound words. (2 Tim. 1:13)
27. The Lord is a ___ of war. (Exod. 15:3)
30. Why sit we ___ until we die? (2 Kings 7:3)
31. Son of Jether. (1 Chron. 7:38)
32. Dignitary's vehicle.
33. Hoosier state (abbr.).
34. Son of Helem. (1 Chron. 7:35)
35. Son of Seth. (Luke 3:38)
36. Angle formed by the junction of stalk and stem.
37. For ye pay tithe of mint and ___. (Matt. 23:23)
38. Father of Abdon. (Judg. 12:13)
41. To the moles and to the ___. (Isa. 2:20)
42. Blue-pencil.
43. Hebrew month.
45. And his ___ was among the thick boughs. (Ezek. 31:3)
48. It is a ___ thing that the king requireth. (Dan. 2:11)
49. Aviation (comb. form).
50. The poor man had nothing, save one little ___. (2 Sam. 12:3)
51. For every man shall ___ his own burden. (Gal. 6:5)
52. And I caused it to ___ upon one city. (Amos 4:7)
53. The shield of his mighty men is made ___. (Nah. 2:3)

Down

1. But the other holy offerings ___ they in pots. (2 Chron. 35:13)
2. Town of Benjamin. (1 Chron. 8:12)
3. I saw the ram pushing ___. (Dan. 8:4)
4. Cereal grass fungi.
5. The priests thereof teach for ___. (Mic. 3:11)
6. Father of Bezaleel. (Exod. 31:2)
7. For the things which are seen are ___. (2 Cor. 4:18)
8. Son of Bani. (Ezra 10:29)
9. But the Lord is in his ___ temple. (Hab. 2:20)
10. Lily.
11. Also such as wrought iron and brass to ___ the house of the Lord. (2 Chron. 24:12)
19. Woe to them that are at ___ in Zion. (Amos 6:1)
21. For it is a ___ of consecration. (Exod. 29:22)
22. Thou shalt call me ___. (Hos. 2:16)
23. Youth.
24. No mention shall be made of ___. (Job. 28:18)
26. My ___ friends have forgotten me. (Job 19:14)
27. That it may ___ grace unto the hearers. (Eph. 4:29)

28. Gatherer of sycomore fruit. (Amos 7:14)

29. He shall not approach . . . he that hath a flat ___. (Lev. 21:18)

32. I have neither ___ on usury. (Jer. 15:10)

34. Shall the ___ boast itself against him that heweth therewith? (Isa. 10:15)

36. Nor ___ the thing that is gone out of my lips. (Ps. 89:34)

37. Made golden calf. (Exod. 32)

38. To cause the bud of the tender ___ to spring forth? (Job 38:27)

39. Members of the family of (suff.).

40. Israeli pound.

41. Italian port city.

44. ___ doubtless, and I count all things but loss. (Phil. 3:8)

46. ___ no man any thing. (Rom. 13:8)

47. Natural soil aggregate.

34

Across

1. After I have been there, I must also see ___. (Acts 19:21)
5. ___ ye not what the scripture saith of Elias? (Rom. 11:2)
8. Ten women shall ___ your bread in one oven. (Lev. 26:26)
12. The Ahohite. (1 Chron. 11:29)
13. And the LORD said, Behold, the people is ___. (Gen. 11:6)
14. Son of Rehoboam. (1 Chron. 3:10)
15. One of the seven churches. (Rev. 2:12)
17. They spread Absalom a ___ upon the top of the house. (2 Sam. 16:22)
18. N.T. book (abbr.).
19. For I know not to give flattering ___. (Job 32:22)
21. He hath put down the mighty from their ___. (Luke 1:52)
24. Prison (Brit.).
25. Love no false ___. (Zech. 8:17)
26. All the people that were with Joab ___ the wall. (2 Sam. 20:15)
30. Father of Josaphat. (Matt. 1:8)
31. Esh- ___, city of refuge. (Josh. 21:14)
32. And I took the little book . . . and ___ it up. (Rev. 10:10)
33. Father of Gamaliel. (Num. 1:10)
35. And these are the sons of Shuthelah: of ___. (Num. 26:36)
36. I will ___ their backsliding, I will love them freely. (Hos. 14:4)
37. The kisses of an ___ are deceitful. (Prov. 27:6)
38. Eleazar's father-in-law. (Exod. 6:25)
41. I ___ daily with you teaching in the temple. (Matt. 26:55)
42. Tribe. (Luke 2:36)
43. For the ___ have emptied them out. (Nah. 2:2)
48. Church part.
49. The sons of ___ were sons of Belial. (1 Sam. 2:12)
50. Goddess of epic poetry.
51. Belonging to the son of Abia. (Matt. 1:7)
52. Latitude (abbr.).
53. Whirlpool.

Down

1. And ___ up their women with child. (2 Kings 8:12)
2. Spanish cheer.
3. And images of your mice that ___ the land. (1 Sam. 6:5)
4. And spared not the old world, but saved Noah the ___ person. (2 Peter 2:5)
5. Out of whose ___ came the ice? (Job 38:29)
6. Benjamite town.
7. It is of no strength at all while the ___ liveth. (Heb. 9:17)
8. Every ___ of the warrior is with confused noise. (Isa. 9:5)
9. Brought of the firstlings of his flock. (Gen. 4:4)
10. Hear this word, ye ___ of Bashan. (Amos 4:1)
11. Consumes.
16. Bronze.
20. Particle.
21. He is like a refiner's fire and like a fuller's ___. (Mal. 3:2)
22. Take thine ___, eat, drink and be merry. (Luke 12:19)
23. They came to the threshingfloor of ___. (Gen. 50:10)
24. Received the twenty-second lot. (1 Chron. 24:17)
26. Made the ark. (Exod. 37:1)
27. It is a ___ thing that the king requireth. (Dan. 2:11)
28. Where Samson lived. (Judg. 15:8)
29. Lest I be full and ___ thee. (Prov. 30:9)
31. Unto ___, O LORD, do I lift up my soul. (Ps. 25:1)

34. Belonging to the son of Enan. (Num. 1:15)
35. Thou shalt ___ him, and thou shalt also prevail. (2 Chron. 18:21)
37. And let me not ___ of their dainties. (Ps. 141:4)
38. Para-amino-benzoic acid (abbr.).
39. Learn to maintain good works for necessary ___. (Titus 3:14)
40. The troops of ___ looked. (Job 6:19)
41. And shall ___ upon him, and shall kill him. (Mark 10:34)
44. Member of the legislative assembly (abbr.).
45. Old age (abbr.).
46. I will ___ you out of their bondage. (Exod. 6:6)
47. Small herb.

35

Across

1. Her ___ was to light on a part of the field. (Ruth 2:3)
4. And he ___ and touched his tongue. (Mark 7:33)
8. Let your speech be alway with grace, seasoned with ___. (Col. 4:6)
12. Period.
13. Bind the ___ of thine head upon thee. (Ezek. 24:17)
14. Let ours also learn to maintain good works for necessary ___. (Tit. 3:14)
15. Sweet spice. (Exod. 30:34)
17. Fastener.
18. Father of Sychem. (Acts 7:16)
19. Whom all ___ and the world worshippeth. (Acts 19:27)
21. ___ in the Lord and wait patiently for him. (Ps. 37:7)
24. Son of Beriah. (1 Chron. 8:16)
27. Is the seed yet in the ___? (Hag. 2:19)
30. Canaanite king. (Num. 21:1)
32. Greek letter.
33. But he is a Jew which is ___ inwardly. (Rom. 2:29)
34. How long shall this man be a ___ unto us? (Exod. 10:7)
35. American industrialist, Eleuthere Irenee DuPont (initials).
36. Therefore shall he ___ in harvest and have nothing. (Prov. 20:4)
37. Son of Cosam. (Luke 3:28)
38. Tool used for splitting cask staves.
39. All the fish of the rivers shall ___ unto thy scales. (Ezek. 29:4)
41. Thou shalt make fifty loops on the ___ of the one curtain. (Exod. 26:10)
43. I thought it good to ___ the signs and wonders. (Dan. 4:2)
45. And I will ___ me up a faithful priest. (1 Sam. 2:35)
49. No one of these shall fail, none shall want her ___. (Isa. 34:16)
51. To whom the mist of darkness is ___ for ever. (2 Peter 2:17)
54. Belonging to the first female.
55. Agave.
56. Lager.
57. Pastry.
58. Four gills.
59. Chinese dynasty.

Down

1. The king's chamberlain. (Esther 2:3)
2. Where Balak brought Balaam from. (Num. 23:7)
3. And pour it into the ___ of his own left hand. (Lev. 14:15)
4. I may tell all my bones: they look and ___ upon me. (Ps. 22:17)
5. Will men take a ___ of it to hang any vessel thereon? (Ezek. 15:3)
6. Son of Caleb. (1 Chron. 4:15)
7. Son of Ishmael. (Gen. 25:15)
8. Belonging to Gaddi's father. (Num. 13:11)
9. Great and noble man. (Ezra 4:10)
10. Grassland.
11. Recipe amount.
16. How can a man be ___ when he is old? (John 3:4)
20. Who is on my ___? who? (2 Kings 9:32)
22. The number of whom is as the ___ of the sea. (Rev. 20:8)
23. Dwell and ___ ye therein and get you possessions therein. (Gen. 34:10)
25. Uzzah and ___, the sons of Abinadab, drave the new cart. (2 Sam. 6:3)
26. ___ them in the clay. (Jer. 43:9)
27. Floats.
28. For he is cast into ___ [2 words] by his own feet. (Job 18:8)
29. These sought their ___ among those reckoned by genealogy. (Ezra 2:62)
31. Like the Gaza or Zin.

34. Even for mine own ___, will I do it. (Isa. 48:11)
38. I will ___ no evil: for thou art with me. (Ps. 23:4)
40. The ___ was brought unto the king's office. (2 Chron. 24:11)
42. ___ ye one another with an holy kiss. (1 Cor. 16:20)
44. He uttereth his mischievous desire: so they ___ it up. (Mic. 7:3)
46. Babylonian district. (Isa. 37:13)
47. Send ye the lamb to the ruler of the land from ___. (Isa. 16:1)

48. Yet shalt thou be brought down with the trees of ___. Ezek. 31:18)
49. And found the colt . . . in a place where two ways ___. (Mark 11:4)
50. District near Babylon. (2 Kings 17:24)
52. He said, "What meaneth the noise of this tumult?" (1 Sam. 4:14)
53. For God sent not his ___ into the world to condemn the world. (John 3:17)

36

Across

1. Their wine is . . . the cruel ___ of asps. (Deut. 32:33)
6. Ephesian goddess. (Acts 19:35)
11. Also the standing corn, with the vineyards and ___. (Judg. 15:5)
13. The seed is ___ under their clods. (Joel 1:17)
14. And how dieth the ___ man? as the fool. (Eccles. 2:16)
15. Let it not be that outward adorning of plaiting the ___. (1 Peter 3:3)
17. This was Simon's work.
18. It was ordained by ___ in the hand of a mediator. (Gal. 3:19)
20. And these made war with ___, King of Sodom. (Gen. 14:2)
21. Moreover take thou unto thee an iron ___. (Ezek. 4:3)
23. (Joseph) gave them a possession in the land of Egypt . . . in the land of ___. (Gen. 47:11)
25. Amorite king. (Josh. 2:10)
26. Each one for himself to worship, to the moles and to the ___. (Isa. 2:20)
27. And a superscription also was written over him in letters of Greek and ___. (Luke 23:38)
30. The men of Chozeba and Joash and ___. (1 Chron. 4:22)
32. Neither can they ___ [2 words] us, that would come from thence. (Luke 16:26)
33. Those that do pitch next unto him shall be the ___ of Issachar. (Num. 2:5)
34. Series of short posts.
35. Credit note (abbr.).
36. And he shall ___ thee in all thy gates. (Deut. 28:52)
38. ___ gave of the tree and I did eat. (Gen. 3:12)
39. It had three ___ in the mouth of it. (Dan. 7:5)

41. ___ his son, whom Tilgathpilneser . . . carried away captive. (1 Chron. 5:6)
43. Son of Jether. (1 Chron. 7:38)
44. Son of Jaaziah. (1 Chron. 24:26)
45. Wrap a dead body.
48. Kind of lens.
50. Salute Philologus, and Julia, ___ and his sister. (Rom. 16:15)
52. The harvest is past, the summer is ___. (Jer. 8:20)
53. Spurn.

Down

1. But for a ___ it shall not be accepted. (Lev. 22:23)
2. Now ___ was ninety and eight years old. (1 Sam. 4:15)
3. Jewish month. (Neh. 2:1)
4. Which to day is, and to morrow is cast into the ___. (Matt. 6:30)
5. Saul, Saul, why persecutest thou ___? (Acts 9:4)
6. In all the region of ___. (1 Kings 4:11)
7. This woman's child died in the night, because she overlaid ___. (1 Kings 3:19)
8. Certifies.
9. For the day of the LORD is ___. (Obad 15)
10. Prophetess of Aser. (Luke 2:36)
12. Put up thy sword into the ___. (John 18:11)
13. And the dead in Christ shall ___ first. (1 Thess. 4:16)
16. Now after many years I came to bring ___ to my nation. (Acts 24:17)
19. I found Israel like ___ in the wilderness. (Hos. 9:10)
20. I was as a ___ before thee. (Ps. 73:22)
21. Eli the priest sat upon a seat by a ___. (1 Sam. 1:9)
22. For this ___ is mount Sinai in Arabia. (Gal. 4:25)

24. Large crustacean.
26. An instructor of the foolish, a teacher of ___. (Rom. 2:20)
28. The Lord will smite thee . . . with the ___. (Deut. 28:27)
29. Give ___ occasion to the adversary to speak reproachfully. (1 Tim. 5:14)
31. Put upon the fringe of the borders a ___ of blue. (Num. 15:38)
32. She shall bring . . . a young ___ for a sin offering. (Lev. 12:6)
34. It had ___ good for that man if he had not ___ born. (Matt. 26:24)
37. Goat.
38. All we like ___ have gone astray. (Isa. 53:6)

39. Let us run with patience the ___ that is set before us. (Heb. 12:1)
40. His bones are like bars of ___. (Job 40:18)
42. Within as it were an half ___ of land. (1 Sam. 14:14)
44. Upon a lofty and high mountain hast thou set thy ___. (Isa. 57:7)
46. Ye tithe mint and ___ and all manner of herbs. (Luke 11:42)
47. English as a second language (abbr.).
49. Day which ended war in European theater.
51. Son of Judah. (Gen. 38:3)

37

Across

1. I do set my ___ in the cloud. (Gen. 9:13)
4. City of Lycia. (Acts 27:5)
8. Muppim, Huppim and ___. (Gen. 46:21)
11. Wing.
12. Artery (comb. form).
13. Thy ___ is not waxen old. (Deut. 29:5)
14. That the ___ of men might seek after the Lord. (Acts 15:17)
16. City of Judah. (2 Sam. 6:2)
17. Town of Palestine. (Josh. 11:2)
18. Used again.
19. Philistine idol. (Judg. 16:23)
22. Son of Reuben. (Exod. 6:14)
23. Ancient Greek coin.
24. Perfumed powder.
25. ___ for ___, tooth for tooth. (Exod. 21:24)
28. ___ Aviv, Israel.
29. Siren.
30. Will a man ___ God? (Mal. 3:8)
31. Old times.
32. Orphanage (abbr.).
33. Timnah or Alvah. (Gen. 36:40)
34. Polynesian island.
36. Lewd fellows of the ___ sort. (Acts 17:5)
37. I defy the ___ of Israel. (1 Sam. 17:10)
39. And it is yet ___ more evident. (Heb. 7:15)
40. Child (Scot.).
41. Foolish and ___ lusts. (1 Tim. 6:9)
45. Computer data.
46. Mine eye hath ___ his desire. (Ps. 54:7)
47. Loyal to David. (1 Kings 1:8)
48. He planteth an ___. (Isa. 44:14)
49. Mourning as the ___. (Mic. 1:8)
50. He laid hold on the dragon, that ___ serpent. (Rev. 20:2)

Down

1. Let them shut the doors, and ___ them. (Neh. 7:3)
2. Well done!
3. And the Word ___ with God. (John 1:1)
4. Jobab's kingdom. (Josh. 11:1)
5. Possessed by you.
6. Rural route east (abbr.).
7. This evil is happened unto you, as ___ this day. (Jer. 44:23)
8. King of Persia. (Esther 1:1)
9. Part.
10. Whatsoever ye do in word or ___. (Col. 3:17)
13. Enquire in the house of Judas for one called ___ of Tarsus. (Acts 9:11)
15. Is this man Coniah a despised, broken ___? (Jer. 22:28)
16. Behold, they ___ out with their mouth. (Ps. 59:7)
18. Musician, ___ Carmichael.
19. And they shall ___. (Jer. 50:36)
20. And of country village, even unto the great stone of ___. (1 Sam. 6:18)
21. So the carpenter encouraged the ___. (Isa. 41:7)
22. South American prairie.
24. Novices.
26. For my ___ is easy, and my burden is light. (Matt. 11:30)
27. Salah lived thirty years and begat ___. (Gen. 11:14)
29. Ancient Roman.
33. It shall be stoned, or thrust through with a ___. (Heb. 12:20)
35. English river.
36. So shall thy ___ be filled with plenty. (Prov. 3:10)
37. Whereby we cry, ___, Father. (Rom. 8:15)
38. Beams.
39. Thou shalt be for ___ to the fire. (Ezek. 21:32)

1	2	3	■	4	5	6	7	■	8	9	10
11				12				13			
14			15				16				
■			17				18				
19	20	21			■	22					■
23				24					25	26	27
28			29						30		
31			32					33			
■		34	35				36				
37	38				39				■		
40					41			42	43	44	
45			46				47				
48			49				50				

41. ___ ye down trees. (Jer. 6:6)
42. Wilt thou break a leaf driven to and ___? (Job 13:25)
43. Son of Bani. (Ezra 10:34)

44. Jehoida . . . bored a hole in the ___ of it. (2 Kings 12:9)
46. As he thinketh in his heart ___ is he. (Prov. 23:7)

38

Across

1. But God commendeth his ___ toward us. (Rom. 5:8)
2. Ye are the ___ of the earth. (Matt. 5:13)
9. Abram's wife. (Gen. 11:29)
14. All they which dwelt in ___ heard the word. (Acts 19:10)
15. Through ___ will we push down our enemies. (Ps. 44:5)
16. Embrace.
17. But covet earnestly the ___ gifts. (1 Cor. 12:31)
18. He sent ___ unto his people. (Ps. 111:9)
20. Loyal to David. (1 Kings 1:8)
21. Let them shut the doors and ___ them. (Neh. 7:3)
22. The ___ of truth shall be established for ever. (Prov. 12:19)
23. Meadow.
24. Before I was afflicted I went ___. (Ps. 119:67)
26. Father of Amminadab. (Ruth 4:19)
28. Which ___ him in the killing of his brethren. (Judg. 9:24)
30. But the Jews ___ up the devout and honourable women. (Acts 13:50)
34. Saturated (abbr.).
36. For in ___ there is no remembrance of thee. (Ps. 6:5)
38. Bristly, springy plant part.
39. Mother of Hezekiah. (2 Kings 18:1, 2)
40. Greek letter.
41. Pen.
42. We know that an ___ is nothing in the world. (1 Cor. 8:4)
44. Son of Zorobabel. (Matt. 1:13)
46. What the navy of Tharshish brought. (1 Kings 10:22)
47. Because he was of the house and ___ of David. (Luke 2:4)
49. And he asked for a writing ___. (Luke 1:63)
51. Musical syllable.
52. Son of Zerah. (1 Chron. 2:6)
55. He planteth an ___, and the rain doth nourish it. (Isa. 44:14)
58. I ___ no pleasant bread. (Dan. 10:3)
60. Bed.
61. And ___ the kine to the cart. (1 Sam. 6:7)
62. Helpful Levite. (Ezra 10:15)
65. Darius the ___. (Dan. 11:1)
66. Bohemian or Polish dance.
67. What do ye, loosing the ___? (Mark 11:5)
68. A certain porter. (Ezra 2:42)
69. He stumbleth not, because he ___ the light. (John 11:9)
70. Groweth unto an ___ temple in the Lord. (Eph. 2:21)
71. Carriage.

Down

1. Insect lips.
2. Belonging to a certain minor prophet. (Rom. 9:25)
3. Glorify God in the day of ___. (1 Peter 2:12)
4. Yet the dogs ___ of the crumbs which fall. (Matt. 15:27)
5. Rambled.
6. The sons of ___. (1 Chron. 7:12)
7. I being in the way, the LORD ___ me. (Gen. 24:27)
8. Sesame.
9. A Philistine giant. (1 Chron. 20:4)
10. Go to the ___, thou sluggard. (Prov. 6:6)
11. He wrote also letters to ___ on the LORD God. (2 Chron. 32:17)
12. Be thou like ___ [2 words] or a young hart. (Song of Sol. 2:17)
13. Son of Helem. (1 Chron. 7:35)
19. And the end of that ___ is heaviness. (Prov. 14:13)
21. The priest shall value it, whether it be good or ___. (Lev. 27:12)
25. I will ___ you out of their bondage. (Exod. 6:6)
27. Married woman's title.
29. And there accompanied him into Asia . . . Gaius of ___. (Acts 20:4)
30. I will punish the fruit of the ___ heart of the king. (Isa. 10:12)
31. He ___ not any that are wise of heart. (Job 37:24)
32. Little one (suff.).

33. My ___ are swifter than a weaver's shuttle. (Job 7:6)
34. For Paul had determined to ___ by Ephesus. (Acts 20:16)
35. Father of Kish. (2 Chron. 29:12)
37. Son of Shamer. (1 Chron. 7:34)
43. ___ not them that wait on thee . . . be ashamed. (Ps. 69:6)
44. Fine linen, coral, and ___. (Ezek. 27:16)
45. Robbery by gangs.
46. That thy profiting may appear to ___. (1 Tim. 4:15)
48. And passed along toward the side over against ___ northward. (Josh. 18:18)

50. And the stork, the heron after her kind, and the lapwing, and the ___. (Lev. 11:19)
53. Superfamily (comb. form).
54. Wary.
55. The poison of ___ is under their lips. (Rom. 3:13)
56. Over Edom will I cast out my ___. (Ps. 60:8)
57. Lest he ___ thee to the judge. (Luke 12:58)
59. Engrave.
60. And ___ upon me in the day of trouble. (Ps. 50:15)
63. Basket (abbr.).
64. Exclamation of surprise.
65. Celebration (comb. form).

39

Across

1. All that dwelt at Lydda and ___ saw him. (Acts 9:35)
6. Chepharhaammonai and Ophni and ___. (Josh. 18:24)
10. Son of Joktan. (1 Chron. 1:22)
14. Son of Gad. (Gen. 46:16)
15. And for it came up four notable ___. (Dan. 8:8)
16. Building toy.
17. My ___ are kindled together. (Hos. 11:8)
19. Interjection.
20. Transportation mode.
21. East Indian unit of weight.
22. I would hasten my ___ from the windy storm and tempest. (Ps. 55:8)
24. On the wall of ___ he built much. (2 Chron. 27:3)
26. In vain have I ___ your children. (Jer. 2:30)
27. Of a certain tower whose top may reach unto heaven. (Gen. 11:4)
29. I forgave thee all that ___ because thou desiredst me. (Matt. 18:32)
30. They of ___ salute you. (Heb. 13:24)
31. Saul died and ___ reigned in his stead. (Gen. 36:38)
36. ___ -a-tete.
37. Out of the ___ of hell cried I. (Jonah 2:2)
38. City from tribe of Benjamin. (Josh. 21:17)
39. Abnormal responses to stimulation.
41. Shrewd.
42. Old dice game.
43. And ___ I was speaking and praying and confessing my sin. (Dan. 9:20)
44. And when thou ___, forgive. (1 Kings 8:30)
48. Girl's name.
49. What ___ thee now. (Isa. 22:1)
50. Native of Helsinki.
51. Lout.

54. And flay their ___ from off them. (Mic. 3:3)
55. Now unto him that is able to do exceeding ___. (Eph. 3:20)
58. Leaping amphibian.
59. River in Egypt.
60. Anoint.
61. River joining the Danube.
62. And he ___ his birthright unto Jacob. (Gen. 25:33)
63. ___ -land, country on the North Sea.

Down

1. Flesh (comb. form).
2. District.
3. God gave them over to a ___ mind. (Rom. 1:28)
4. Heard at bull fights.
5. In the ninth place.
6. It shall ___ [2 words] with him that is left in his tabernacle. (Job 20:26)
7. There was one ___, a prophetess, the daughter of Phanuel. (Luke 2:36)
8. Therefore shall he ___ in harvest, and have nothing. (Prov. 20:4)
9. There come unto your ___ a man with a gold ring. (James 2:2)
10. Put on therefore, as the ___ of God. (Col. 3:12)
11. Hearken unto thy father that ___ thee. (Prov. 23:22)
12. God's love.
13. Thick woolen cloth.
18. Having their thumbs and great ___ cut off, [the kings] gathered their meat under my table. (Judg. 1:7)
23. ___ thou hast not hated blood, even blood shall pursue me. (Ezek. 35:6)
25. Son of Jahdai. (1 Chron. 2:47)
26. The Lamb opened one of the ___. (Rev. 6:1)
27. Surely the serpent will ___ without enchantment. (Eccles. 10:11)
28. A certain porter. (Ezra 2:42)

29. ___ -nutha, by the sea of Galilee. (Mark 8:10)
31. And the sin which doth so easily ___ us. (Heb. 12:1)
32. And ___, I will put my trust in him. (Heb. 2:13)
33. Their widows were ___ in the daily ministration. (Acts 6:1)
34. Certain insect (2 words). (Isa. 7:18)
35. Denials.
37. Belonging to a Jew of the captivity. (Ezra 2:2)
40. Small quantity (Scot.)
41. When he had destroyed seven nations in the land of ___. (Acts 13:19)

43. Their molten images are ___ and confusion. (Isa. 41:29)
44. O my strength, ___ thee to help me. (Ps. 22:19)
45. Image.
46. Son of Shobal. (1 Chron. 1:40)
47. Rips.
48. So when they had ___, Jesus saith . . . lovest thou me more than these? (John 21:15)
50. Woe unto you that are ___! (Luke 6:25)
52. All (Ger.).
53. One who colors fabrics.
56. Life story (shortened form).
57. Compass point.

40

Across

1. Ye hypocrites, ye can discern the face of the ___. (Luke 12:56)
4. Let their table be made a snare and a ___. (Rom. 11:9)
8. Or ___ his jaw through with a thorn? (Job 41:2)
12. There shall they ___ in a good fold. (Ezek. 34:14)
13. Keeper of the women. (Esther 2:3)
14. Father of Peleg and Joktan. (Gen. 10:25)
15. Whosoever shall kill shall be ___ danger of the judgment. (Matt. 5:21)
16. Spanish dance.
18. American humorist, George ___.
19. But the talk of the lips tendeth only to ___. (Prov. 14:23)
21. But delivered him up for us ___. (Rom. 8:32)
23. Jar.
24. And when they did ___ it with an omer. (Exod. 16:18)
26. ___ also are men of like passions with you. (Acts 14:15)
28. And hide them in the clay in the brick- ___. (Jer. 43:9)
30. But if he wash them not, nor ___ his flesh. (Lev. 17:16)
31. His bed was nine cubits long. (Deut. 3:11)
32. Love worketh no ___ to his neighbour. (Rom. 13:10)
33. For ___ hath forsaken me, having loved this present world. (2 Tim. 4:10)
34. I cannot dig; to ___ I am ashamed. (Luke 16:3)
35. Musical syllable.
36. But God prepared ___ [2 words] when the morning rose. (Jonah 4:7)
37. And there followed him a ___ of meat from the king. (2 Sam. 11:8)
38. Chinese unit of distance.
39. Thou hast bought me no sweet ___ with money. (Isa. 43:24)
40. I will liken him unto a wise ___. (Matt. 7:24)
41. Steamer (abbr.).
42. Ask ye of the LORD rain in the time of the ___ rain. (Zech. 10:1)
45. Yet what I shall choose I ___ not. (Phil. 1:22)
47. And there was a sore ___ in Samaria. (1 Kings 18:2)
50. Behold I will punish the multitude of ___. (Jer. 46:25)
51. ___, Eschol and Mamre; let them take their portion. (Gen. 14:24)
53. They escaped all ___ to land. (Acts 27:44)
54. But the other holy offerings ___ they in pots. (2 Chron. 35:13)
55. When he was in ___ he sought me out. (2 Tim. 1:17)
56. Adrenocorticotrophic hormone (abbr.).
57. But this ___ thing I do. (Phil. 3:13)

Down

1. Lest at any time we should let them ___. (Heb. 2:1)
2. Hear ye this word, ye ___ of Bashan. (Amos 4:1)
3. ___ are all the children of light. (1 Thess. 5:5)
4. As a ___ goeth up into the hand of a drunkard. (Prov. 26:9)
5. Because thou didst ___ on the LORD, he delivered them into thine hand. (2 Chron. 16:8)
6. If she pass the flower of her ___. (1 Cor. 7:36)
7. Through.
8. But if ye ___ without chastisement, . . . then are ye bastards and not sons. (Heb. 12:8)
9. And ___ and Abimael and Sheba. (Gen. 10:28)
10. Though they be ___ like crimson, they shall be as wool. (Isa. 1:18)
11. How long will it be ___ they believe me? (Num. 14:11)
16. And they shall both ___ together. (Isa. 1:31)
17. But shalt perform unto the Lord thine ___. (Matt. 5:33)
20. Invalid.
22. Shelter.
24. A plain near Hebron. (Gen. 13:18)
25. He [Samson] went down and dwelt in the top of the rock ___. (Judg. 15:8)

26. There come two ___ more hereafter. (Rev. 9:12)
27. Which leaveth her ___ in the earth and warmeth them in dust. (Job 39:14)
28. Ye ___, and desire to have, and cannot obtain. (James 4:2)
29. The Ahohite (1 Chron. 11:29)
30. Shebam and Nebo and ___. (Num. 32:3)
33. Or crookbackt, or a ___, or that hath a blemish in his eye. (Lev. 21:20)
34. And my people are ___ to backsliding from me. (Hos. 11:7)
36. This woman was taken in adultery, in the very ___. (John 8:4)
37. No one of these shall fail, none shall want her ___. (Isa. 34:16)
40. Twenty shekels, five and twenty shekels, fifteen shekels, shall be your ___. (Ezek. 45:12)
41. There shall come forth a rod out of the ___ of Jesse. (Isa. 11:1)
42. Humble yourselves in the sight of the Lord, and he shall ___ you up. (James 4:10)
43. Where John was baptizing (alternate spelling). (John 3:23)
44. So the posts that ___ upon mules and camels went out. (Esther 8:14)
45. From the bent bow, and from the grievousness of ___. (Isa. 21:15)
46. In some one of the villages in the plain of ___. (Neh. 6:2)
48. Father of Berechiah. (1 Chron. 9:16)
49. Raincoat (Brit.).
52. Second tone on the diatonic scale.
54. King of Egypt. (2 Kings 17:4)

41

Across

1. ___ saith the Holy Ghost. (Acts 21:11)
5. When they heard that, they were ___ to the heart. (Acts 5:33)
8. A man that beareth false witness against his neighbour is a ___. (Prov. 25:18)
12. The Lord GOD will ___ away tears from off all faces. (Isa. 25:8)
13. King of Judah. (1 Kings 15:8)
14. That where I am, there ye may be ___. (John 14:3)
15. Potipherah, priest of ___ bare unto him. (Gen. 41:50)
16. The cedars of ___ which he hath planted. (Ps. 104:16)
19. ___ al (and others).
20. Like the first element of the word. (suff.).
21. I will make Jerusalem heaps, and a ___ of dragons. (Jer. 9:11)
23. King Zedekiah sent unto him ___ the son of Melchiah. (Jer. 21:1)
26. Belonging to the chancellor. (Ezra 4:9)
29. Less-than-truckload lot (abbr.).
30. He ___ me to make me king over all Israel. (1 Chron. 28:4)
32. Mercy and truth are ___ together. (Ps. 85:10)
33. University of Texas at Arlington (abbr.).
34. Mine eye also is ___ by reason of sorrow. (Job 17:7)
35. Bleat.
36. Nathan said to David, Thou art the ___. (2 Sam. 12:7)
37. Of a son of Zophah. (1 Chron. 7:36)
39. Whose ___ is destruction, whose God is their belly. (Phil. 3:19)
40. Jehu's captain. (2 Kings 9:25)
42. And their tongue faileth for ___. (Isa. 41:17)
44. And Jacob ___ pottage. (Gen. 25:29)
45. Mantra sounds.
46. I will see what their end shall ___. (Deut. 32:20)
48. And he shall sit as a ___ and purifier of silver. (Mal. 3:3)
52. Sunday school (abbr.).
54. And certain of the chief of ___. (Acts 19:31)
56. Eldest son of Caleb. (1 Chron. 4:15)
57. Gibeah: and Uzzah and ___ . . . , drave the new cart. (2 Sam. 6:3)
59. Son of Canaan. (Gen. 10:15)
60. And take away all thy ___. (Isa. 1:25)
61. And defiled my ___ in the dust. (Job 16:15)

Down

1. ___ of every sort shalt thou bring into the ark. (Gen. 6:19)
2. The fourth part of an ___ of wine for a drink offering. (Exod. 29:40)
3. All these things have I kept from my youth ___. (Matt. 19:20)
4. Psalmist's pause.
5. Fourth part of a ___ of dove's dung. (2 Kings 6:25)
6. For unto ___ [2 words] child is born. (Isa. 9:6)
7. What Simon would do at work. (Acts 9:43)
8. Twenty shekels, five and twenty shekels, fifteen shekels shall be your ___. (Ezek. 45:12)
9. American League (abbr.).
10. But that which is good to the ___ of edifying. (Eph. 4:29)
11. His ___ was to burn incense. (Luke 1:9)
17. Jewish month. (Neh. 6:15)
18. A prophet of the LORD was there, whose name was ___. (2 Chron. 28:9)
20. I will make the rivers ___. (Isa. 42:15)

22. Part of the Pentateuch.

23. Behold, I will set a ___ -line in the midst of my people. (Amos 7:8)

24. ___ the sixth, Eliel the seventh. (1 Chron. 12:11)

25. She scorneth the horse and his ___. (Job 39:18)

26. Whose soever sins ye ___, they are remitted unto them. (John 20:23)

27. Lest by any ___ I should run, or had run, in vain. (Gal. 2:2)

28. City (Ger.).

31. And carried the people of it captive to ___. (2 Kings 16:9)

37. And the man did as Joseph ___. (Gen. 43:17)

38. A man plucked off his ___ and gave it to his neighbour. (Ruth 4:7)

41. That he be not as ___ and as his company. (Num. 16:40)

43. Brother of 37 across.

46. ___ humbug!

47. Compass point.

49. Is it ___ to say to a king, Thou art wicked? (Job 34:18)

50. Son of Bela. (1 Chron. 7:7)

51. Father of Oshea [Joshua]. (Num. 13:8)

52. And I said unto him, ___, thou knowest. (Rev. 7:14)

53. He that hath the ___ hath life. (1 John 5:12)

55. And God saw the light, that ___ was good. (Gen. 1:4)

58. ___, every one that thirsteth. (Isa. 55:1)

42

Across

1. Brother of Rebekah. (Gen. 24:29)
6. Let us ___ by the same rule. (Phil. 3:16)
10. Afterward he appeared unto the ___. (Mark 16:14)
12. An Ahohite. (1 Chron. 11:29)
13. This ___ in remembrance of me. (Luke 22:19)
14. King of Judah. (1 Kings 15:8)
15. For whom I have suffered the ___ of all things. (Phil. 3:8)
16. Wildebeest.
18. He that ___ the land shall be satisfied with bread. (Prov. 12:11)
20. A ready scribe in the law of Moses. (Ezra 7:6)
22. The idols have spoken vanity, and the diviners have seen a ___. (Zech. 10:2)
23. Stains.
25. Wing (comb. form).
29. And upon the great ___ of their right foot. (Exod. 29:20)
31. Tow.
32. For the children ought not to lay up for the ___. (2 Cor. 12:14)
36. Was not with Adonijah. (1 Kings 1:8)
37. Son of Eliphaz. (Gen. 36:11)
38. Wing.
40. On the back of the page (abbr.).
41. Casting all your ___ upon him. (1 Peter 5:7)
42. Allegorical drama performed by masked actors.
44. Prophet in Samaria. (2 Chron. 28:9)
45. Safe.

Down

1. And the borders were between the ___. (1 Kings 7:28)
2. Masculine personal name.
3. And God said, Let there ___ light. (Gen. 1:3)
4. The king of Assyria brought men from . . . ___. (2 Kings 17:24)
5. Thou puttest thy ___ in a rock. (Num. 24:21)
6. It is not of him that ___ nor of him that runneth. (Rom. 9:16)
7. Lily.
8. The ___ enemy that shall be destroyed is death. (1 Cor. 15:26)
9. And the asses of ___ Saul's father were lost. (1 Sam. 9:3)
11. Sisera lay dead, and the ___ was in his temples. (Judg. 4:22)
17. Geber the son of ___ was in the country of Gilead. (1 Kings 4:19)
19. The ___ of truth shall be established for ever. (Prov. 12:19)
21. As he prayed the fashion of his countenance was ___. (Luke 9:29)
24. And that man of sin be revealed, the ___ of perdition. (2 Thess. 2:3)
26. A liar giveth ___ to a naughty tongue. (Prov. 17:4)
27. Dismal.
28. Then returned they unto Jerusalem from the mount called ___. (Acts 1:12)
30. And he went down and dwelt in the top of the rock ___. (Judg. 15:8)
32. Slightly, musical direction.
33. Town of Asher. (Josh. 19:26)
34. It is a ___ thing that the king requireth. (Dan. 2:11)
35. One whose native language is Slavic.
39. Son of Jether. (1 Chron. 7:38)
43. Queen (abbr.).

43

Across

1. Thou mayest kill and eat flesh in all thy ___. (Deut. 12:15)
6. Our eyelids ___ out with waters. (Jer. 9:18)
10. ___ said unto Jacob, Come near . . . that I may feel thee. (Gen. 27:21)
11. Margarine.
12. Lock.
13. Until the day ___, and the day star arise in your hearts. (2 Peter 1:19)
14. Grunting sound.
15. To make their land desolate and a perpetual ___. (Jer. 18:16)
17. Society of Automotive Engineering Students (abbr.).
19. A child of Gad. (1 Chron. 5:13)
20. For that which I do I ___ not. (Rom. 7:15)
22. Jewish month. (Neh. 2:1)
26. Chose the plain of Jordan. (Gen. 13:11)
28. Wooden groove.
29. Ardent follower.
33. The children of ___, Halid, and Ono. (Ezra 2:33)
34. They came to ___ where there were twelve water wells. (Exod. 15:27)
35. Love affair.
37. Nigerian city.
38. Lasso.
39. Let all the people say, ___. (Ps. 106:48)
40. Representing a palatal stop.

Down

1. Israelite camp. (Josh. 4:19)
2. ___ was as light of foot as a wild roe. (2 Sam. 2:18)
3. Make lace.
4. Let ___ esteem other better than themselves. (Phil. 2:3)
5. Split (comb. form).
6. Yea, hath ___ [2 words], ye shall not eat of every tree of the garden. (Gen. 3:1)
7. River of Chaldea. (Dan. 8:2)
8. Basted.
9. ___ Kong.
14. Land of the free.
16. Tempted like as we are, yet without ___. (Heb. 4:15)
18. ___ in all his glory was not arrayed like one of these. (Matt. 6:29)
21. Yet what I shall choose I ___ not. (Phil. 1:22)
23. ___ no man by the way. (Luke 10:4)
24. And ___ was over the tribute. (2 Sam. 20:24)
25. Where Cain lived. (Gen. 4:16)
27. I water my couch with my ___. (Ps. 6:6)
29. Ten (comb. form).
30. Israelite chief. (Neh. 10:14)
31. I am the ___, ye are the branches. (John 15:5)
32. In the blood (comb. form).
36. Grain.

90

44

Across

1. And maketh collops of ___ on his flanks. (Job 15:27)
4. Fuel.
7. His mother's name was ___, the daughter of Zachariah. (2 Kings 18:2)
10. Son of Bela. (1 Chron. 7:7)
11. How art thou fallen from heaven, O ___. (Isa. 14:12)
13. But avoid foolish questions and ___. (Titus 3:9)
15. One of the twelve tribes. (Num. 1:25)
16. Unusually early (archaic).
17. She ___ in her body that she was healed of that plague. (Mark 5:29)
19. International Center for Learning (abbr.).
20. Believe me that I am ___ the Father, and the Father in me. (John 14:11)
22. And Abimelech took an ___ in his hand. (Judg. 9:48)
23. He planteth an ___ and the rain doth nourish it. (Isa. 44:14)
24. Mother of all living. (Gen. 3:20)
25. Second tone of diatonic scale.
26. Father of Josaphat. (Matt. 1:8)
27. Twosome.
28. Nathanael's home. (John 21:2)
30. Vase.
31. And ___ I will multiply thee. (Heb. 6:14)
35. What makes a felucca fast. (2 words)
36. Signal.
37. ___ volente, Latin for God being willing.
38. High-power amplifier (abbr.).
39. Within (comb. form).

Down

1. Can the ___ tree, my brethren, bear olive berries? (James 3:12)
2. Your riches ___ corrupted. (James 5:2)
3. The ears of everyone that heareth it shall ___. (1 Sam. 3:11)
4. I will be ___ in the LORD. (Ps. 104:34)
5. His master shall bore his ear through with an ___. (Exod. 21:6)
6. Power was given unto him to ___ men with fire. (Rev. 16:8)
7. Shall send him away by the hand of ___ [2 words] man. (Lev. 16:21)
8. What the carcase of the lion became. (Judg. 14:8)
9. Internal Revenue Service (abbr.).
12. Son of Joseph. (Num. 13:7)
14. The lion shall ___ straw like the ox. (Isa. 11:7)
17. But their heart is ___ from me. (Matt. 15:8)
18. A revenger to ___ wrath upon him that doeth evil. (Rom. 13:4)
19. Major prophet (abbr.).
21. They have prepared a ___ for my steps. (Ps. 57:6)
23. A Shilonite. (1 Chron. 9:5)
24. Timothy's mother. (2 Tim. 1:5)
26. The ___ are a people not strong. (Prov. 30:25)
27. Let it now be ___ only upon the fleece. (Judg. 6:39)
29. So faith without works is dead ___. (James 2:26)
30. Father of Haniel. (1 Chron. 7:39)
31. Central.
32. British army captain's insignia.
33. Father of Joshua (Oshea). (Num. 13:16).
34. ___ thee behind me, Satan. (Matt. 16:23)

45

Across

1. Ehud's father. (Judg. 3:15)
5. And I will ___ them upon their land. (Amos. 9:15)
10. Egyptian sun disk.
14. Son of Dishan. (Gen. 36:28)
15. Under the ___ were undersetters molten. (1 Kings 7:30)
16. ___ -burg, West Germany.
17. ___ -dieu, praying desk.
18. City of Naphtali. (Josh. 19:33)
19. And they shall ___ away their ears from the truth. (2 Tim. 4:4)
20. Greek goddess of dawn.
21. I ___ no pleasant bread. (Dan. 10:3)
22. Cultic mantras.
24. Massachusetts Institute of Technology (abbr.).
25. And Joseph ___ a dream. (Gen. 37:5)
27. Moabite city. (1 Sam. 22:3)
29. Minor prophet (abbr.).
30. Amphitheater.
32. Behold, a greater than ___ is here. (Matt. 12:41)
35. ___, who shall live when God doeth this! (Num. 24:23)
36. Whosoever shall say to his brother ___. (Matt. 5:22)
40. For the eyes of the Lord are ___ the righteous. (1 Peter 3:12)
41'. Tilt.
42. Where Joshua built an altar. (Josh. 8:30)
43. Equal to the ephah. (Ezek. 45:11)
44. Father of Zaccur. (Neh. 3:2)
45. Short plant stalk.
46. Israelite camp. (Num. 33:6)
48. Red or Dead.
49. Interjection used to attract attention.
52. The true light now ___. (1 John 2:8)
56. ___ [2 words] lama sabachthani. (Matt. 27:46)
57. Inner (comb. form).
59. Over (poet.).
60. Son of Shamer. (1 Chron. 7:34)
61. Wast called a transgressor from the ___. (Isa. 48:8)
63. Quarrel.
65. And they came to the threshingfloor of ___. (Gen. 50:10)
66. Seth's son. (Gen. 4:26)
67. Nearest (Scot.).
68. ___ , ___ tekel upharsin. (Dan. 5:25)
69. And ye shall find ___ unto your souls. (Matt. 11:29)
70. Social engagements.
71. Annoys.

Down

1. They ___ upon me with their mouths. (Ps. 22:13)
2. Neither say thou before the angel, that it was an ___. (Eccles. 5:6)
3. Thou shalt not ___ a false report. (Exod. 23:1)
4. One.
5. And they did beat the gold into thin ___. (Exod. 39:3)
6. They ___ us with such things as were necessary. (Acts 28:10)
7. District near Babylon. (2 Kings 17:24)
8. ___ me impune lacessit; no one attacks me with impunity.
9. Why ___ thou thy way to seek love? (Jer. 2:33)
10. Astern.
11. With the voice of the archangel and with the ___ of God. (1 Thess. 4:16)
12. Scary.
13. The ___ captain for the ninth month was Abiezer. (2 Chron. 27:12)
21. Herdman prophet.
23. Stand in awe and ___ not. (Ps. 4:4)
26. Son of Harum. (1 Chron. 4:8)
28. City located near Adam. (Josh. 3:16)
30. Sound an ___ in my holy mountain. (Joel 2:1)
31. Hindu queen.
32. Perfect, upright man who eschewed evil.
33. Eggs.
34. As a wild bull in a ___. (Isa. 51:20)

35. ___ mater.
37. Daughter of Zachariah. (2 Kings 18:2)
38. Beret.
39. Beer.
41. The LORD shall do unto them as he did to ___ [2 words] to Og. (Deut. 31:4)
45. Mountain Israelites journeyed past. (Deut. 2:1)
47. Upon the great ___ of their right foot. (Exod. 29:20)
48. Then ye shall give me thirty ___. (Judg. 14:13)
49. From the ___ of thy wood unto the drawer of thy water. (Deut. 29:11)

50. It is not good that man should be ___. (Gen. 2:18)
51. Chauffeur-driven cars.
52. Pickle.
53. Out of the ___ came forth meat. (Judg. 14:14)
54. We are bound to ___ God always for you. (2 Thess. 1:3)
55. Conceals.
58. ___ juncta in uno; three joined in one.
62. Bachelor of Sacred Theology (abbr.).
64. Lest Satan should ___ an advantage of us. (2 Cor. 2:11)
65. The children of ___. (Ezra 2:57)

Answers

1

```
C A I N   A N D   A B E L
A L O E   L I E   B E T A
N I T R   I M P   R A T S
A D A G I O   A R A R A T
      A C T   R O D
B A A L A H   T W E L V E
A W L           O I L
D E L U D E   G O R G E D
    S U N   I R I
E N S U E S   L E V I T E
B I E R   I C E   E D E N
A X L E   G O A   R O T O
L E A R   N O D   S L E W
```

4

```
L A W   C L A P   C R A G
A S A   H A L E   H A T E
T I N   A D A R   A M E N
E A T E R   S I N S
      A G E   L E T T E R
S P A R E T H   W E A R E
H A P   C O W   S I S
I T A L Y   T H I C K E T
P E N I E L   O N O
    F A I L   T R O D E
S H U T   N O T E   R A D
E A S E   E V E N   E R E
A T E R   S E N T   B E N
```

2

```
O D D   S H O A   M E A T
L O O   H E R B   E T N A
D E C L A R E   B L A N C
    T I M E   R A A M A H
H O R S E   L E A N
O M I T   E B A L   P S I
S E N S E S   L I G H T S
E R E   A R A M   R I A L
    A G O N   B I L G E
B E C A L M   B A N I
A W A R E   G R A S P E D
B E N O   A N A L   P E A
I R A N   T U N E   I N N
```

5

```
D O E R   C A W   H A T H
E A S E   O W E   A R E A
W R E S T L E   G R I N D
    R I O T   B A B A
A R I S E   D E M O N I C
P A N T   P E T E R   N O
A B E   P A L E S   M A D
R B   F A T A L   J A N E
T I M O T H Y   L A T E X
    O R E S   Q U I Z
W I S E R   B U G L O S S
A C E S   J A I   E T T E
R E S T   O R T   R H E A
```

3

```
L U D   M I D A S   J A Y
I R E   I M A G E   O P A
P E L I C A N   V E N O M
    I R A M   S E L A
D A V A H   D Y N A S T Y
E D E N   N O N T H   R A
I E R   S A V O Y   S E H
S N   A I M E D   S P E W
M O N S T E R   W O R S E
    A I D S   S A R I
A S T R O   D E F E N C E
D U E   W H I N E   G U T
O P S   N A D I R   S E C
```

6

```
A W N   P A L L   T R O P
I O U   A R E A   R O L E
D O M I N I O N   A M E N
    B R E D   G I D E O N
S H E O L   M U S E
T U R N   T O I L S O M E
O L E   M A N S E   N O L
P A D I S H A H   N E C K
    S A I D   D I S K S
F E R R E T   A R T I
A R I A   I N F O R M E R
U N D E   A L A S   U S E
N E E L   N O R S   S T D
```

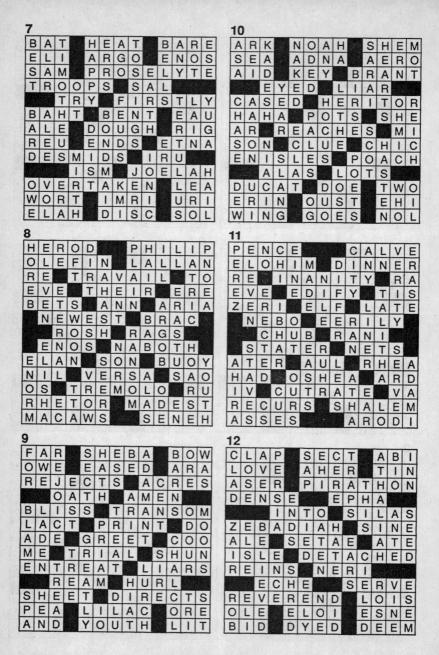

7

B	A	T		H	E	A	T		B	A	R	E
E	L	I		A	R	G	O		E	N	O	S
S	A	M		P	R	O	S	E	L	Y	T	E
T	R	O	O	P	S		S	A	L			
	T	R	Y		F	I	R	S	T	L	Y	
B	A	H	T		B	E	N	T		E	A	U
A	L	E		D	O	U	G	H		R	I	G
R	E	U		E	N	D	S		E	T	N	A
D	E	S	M	I	D	S		I	R	U		
		I	S	M		J	O	E	L	A	H	
O	V	E	R	T	A	K	E	N		L	E	A
W	O	R	T		I	M	R	I		U	R	I
E	L	A	H		D	I	S	C		S	O	L

10

A	R	K		N	O	A	H		S	H	E	M
S	E	A		A	D	N	A		A	E	R	O
A	I	D		K	E	Y		B	R	A	N	T
	E	Y	E	D		L	I	A	R			
C	A	S	E	D		H	E	R	I	T	O	R
H	A	H	A		P	O	T	S		S	H	E
A	R		R	E	A	C	H	E	S		M	I
S	O	N		C	L	U	E		C	H	I	C
E	N	I	S	L	E	S		P	O	A	C	H
		A	L	A	S		L	O	T	S		
D	U	C	A	T		D	O	E		T	W	O
E	R	I	N		O	U	S	T		E	H	I
W	I	N	G		G	O	E	S		N	O	L

8

H	E	R	O	D		P	H	I	L	I	P
O	L	E	F	I	N		L	A	L	L	A	N
R	E		T	R	A	V	A	I	L		T	O
E	V	E		T	H	E	I	R		E	R	E
B	E	T	S		A	N	N		A	R	I	A
	N	E	W	E	S	T		B	R	A	C	
	R	O	S	H		R	A	G	S		
	E	N	O	S		N	A	B	O	T	H
E	L	A	N		S	O	N		B	U	O	Y
N	I	L		V	E	R	S	A		S	A	O
O	S		T	R	E	M	O	L	O		R	U
R	H	E	T	O	R		M	A	D	E	S	T
M	A	C	A	W	S		S	E	N	E	H	

11

P	E	N	C	E		C	A	L	V	E
E	L	O	H	I	M		D	I	N	N	E	R
R	E		I	N	A	N	I	T	Y		R	A
E	V	E		E	D	I	F	Y		T	I	S
Z	E	R	I		E	L	F		L	A	T	E
	N	E	B	O		E	E	R	I	L	Y	
	C	H	U	B		R	A	N	I		
	S	T	A	T	E	R		N	E	T	S
A	T	E	R		A	U	L		R	H	E	A
H	A	D		O	S	H	E	A		A	R	D
I	V		C	U	T	R	A	T	E		V	A
R	E	C	U	R	S		S	H	A	L	E	M
A	S	S	E	S		A	R	O	D	I	

9

F	A	R		S	H	E	B	A		B	O	W
O	W	E		E	A	S	E	D		A	R	A
R	E	J	E	C	T	S		A	C	R	E	S
	O	A	T	H		A	M	E	N		
B	L	I	S	S		T	R	A	N	S	O	M
L	A	C	T		P	R	I	N	T		D	O
A	D	E		G	R	E	E	T		C	O	O
M	E		T	R	I	A	L		S	H	U	N
E	N	T	R	E	A	T		L	I	A	R	S
		R	E	A	M		H	U	R	L		
S	H	E	E	T		D	I	R	E	C	T	S
P	E	A		L	I	L	A	C		O	R	E
A	N	D		Y	O	U	T	H		L	I	T

12

C	L	A	P		S	E	C	T		A	B	I
L	O	V	E		A	H	E	R		T	I	N
A	S	E	R		P	I	R	A	T	H	O	N
D	E	N	S	E		E	P	H	A		
		I	N	T	O		S	I	L	A	S
Z	E	B	A	D	I	A	H		S	I	N	E
A	L	E		S	E	T	A	E		A	T	E
I	S	L	E		D	E	T	A	C	H	E	D
R	E	I	N	S		N	E	R	I		
	E	C	H	E			S	E	R	V	E
R	E	V	E	R	E	N	D		L	O	I	S
O	L	E		E	L	O	I		E	S	N	E
B	I	D		D	Y	E	D		D	E	E	M

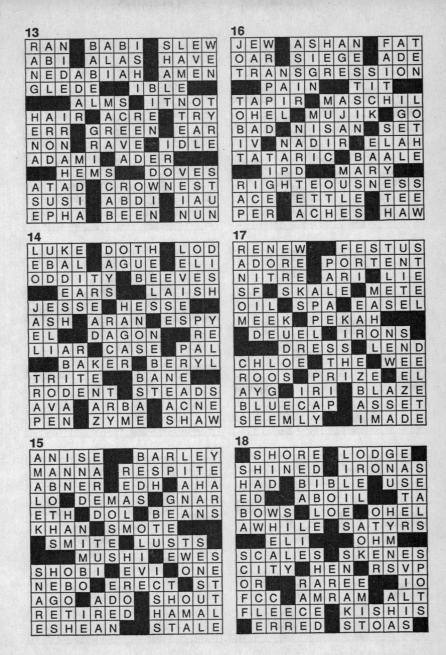

13

R	A	N		B	A	B	I			S	L	E	W
A	B	I		A	L	A	S			H	A	V	E
N	E	D	A	B	I	A	H			A	M	E	N
G	L	E	D	E			I	B	L	E			
			A	L	M	S		I	T	N	O	T	
H	A	I	R		A	C	R	E			T	R	Y
E	R	R		G	R	E	E	N			E	A	R
N	O	N		R	A	V	E		I	D	L	E	
A	D	A	M	I		A	D	E	R				
	H	E	M	S				D	O	V	E	S	
A	T	A	D		C	R	O	W	N	E	S	T	
S	U	S	I		A	B	D	I		I	A	U	
E	P	H	A		B	E	E	N		N	U	N	

16

J	E	W		A	S	H	A	N			F	A	T
O	A	R		S	I	E	G	E		A	D	E	
T	R	A	N	S	G	R	E	S	S	I	O	N	
		P	A	I	N			T	I	T			
T	A	P	I	R		M	A	S	C	H	I	L	
O	H	E	L		M	U	J	I	K		G	O	
B	A	D		N	I	S	A	N		S	E	T	
I	V		N	A	D	I	R		E	L	A	H	
T	A	T	A	R	I	C		B	A	A	L	E	
	I	P	D			M	A	R	Y				
R	I	G	H	T	E	O	U	S	N	E	S	S	
A	C	E		E	T	T	L	E		T	E	E	
P	E	R		A	C	H	E	S		H	A	W	

14

L	U	K	E		D	O	T	H		L	O	D	
E	B	A	L		A	G	U	E		E	L	I	
O	D	D	I	T	Y		B	E	E	V	E	S	
		E	A	R	S			L	A	I	S	H	
J	E	S	S	E		H	E	S	S	E			
A	S	H		A	R	A	N		E	S	P	Y	
E	L		D	A	G	O	N			R	E		
L	I	A	R		C	A	S	E		P	A	L	
	B	A	K	E	R		B	E	R	Y	L		
T	R	I	T	E		B	A	N	E				
R	O	D	E	N	T		S	T	E	A	D	S	
A	V	A		A	R	B	A		A	C	N	E	
P	E	N		Z	Y	M	E		S	H	A	W	

17

R	E	N	E	W			F	E	S	T	U	S	
A	D	O	R	E		P	O	R	T	E	N	T	
N	I	T	R	E		A	R	I		L	I	E	
S	F		S	K	A	L	E		M	E	T	E	
O	I	L		S	P	A		E	A	S	E	L	
M	E	E	K		P	E	K	A	H				
	D	E	U	E	L		I	R	O	N	S		
		D	R	E	S	S		L	E	N	D		
C	H	L	O	E		T	H	E		W	E	E	
R	O	O	S		P	R	I	Z	E		E	L	
A	Y	G		I	R	I		B	L	A	Z	E	
B	L	U	E	C	A	P		A	S	S	E	T	
S	E	E	M	L	Y			I	M	A	D	E	

15

A	N	I	S	E			B	A	R	L	E	Y	
M	A	N	N	A		R	E	S	P	I	T	E	
A	B	N	E	R		E	D	H		A	H	A	
L	O		D	E	M	A	S		G	N	A	R	
E	T	H		D	O	L		B	E	A	N	S	
K	H	A	N		S	M	O	T	E				
	S	M	I	T	E		L	U	S	T	S		
		M	U	S	H	I		E	W	E	S		
S	H	O	B	I		E	V	I		O	N	E	
N	E	B	O		E	R	E	C	T		S	T	
A	G	O		A	D	O		S	H	O	U	T	
R	E	T	I	R	E	D		H	A	M	A	L	
E	S	H	E	A	N		S	T	A	L	E		

18

	S	H	O	R	E		L	O	D	G	E		
S	H	I	N	E	D		I	R	O	N	A	S	
H	A	D		B	I	B	L	E		U	S	E	
E	D		A	B	O	I	L			T	A		
B	O	W	S		L	O	E		O	H	E	L	
A	W	H	I	L	E		S	A	T	Y	R	S	
	E	L	I					O	H	M			
S	C	A	L	E	S		S	K	E	N	E	S	
C	I	T	Y		H	E	N		R	S	V	P	
O	R		R	A	R	E	E			I	O		
F	C	C		A	M	R	A	M		A	L	T	
F	L	E	E	C	E		K	I	S	H	I	S	
	E	R	R	E	D		S	T	O	A	S		

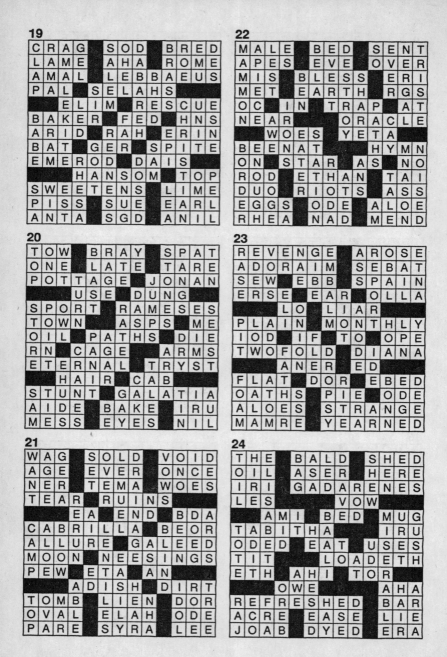

19

C	R	A	G		S	O	D		B	R	E	D
L	A	M	E		A	H	A		R	O	M	E
A	M	A	L		L	E	B	B	A	E	U	S
P	A	L		S	E	L	A	H	S			
	E	L	I	M		R	E	S	C	U	E	
B	A	K	E	R		F	E	D		H	N	S
A	R	I	D		R	A	H		E	R	I	N
B	A	T		G	E	R		S	P	I	T	E
E	M	E	R	O	D		D	A	I	S		
	H	A	N	S	O	M		T	O	P		
S	W	E	E	T	E	N	S		L	I	M	E
P	I	S	S		S	U	E		E	A	R	L
A	N	T	A		S	G	D		A	N	I	L

22

M	A	L	E		B	E	D		S	E	N	T
A	P	E	S		E	V	E		O	V	E	R
M	I	S		B	L	E	S	S		E	R	I
M	E	T		E	A	R	T	H		R	G	S
O	C		I	N		T	R	A	P		A	T
N	E	A	R			O	R	A	C	L	E	
	W	O	E	S		Y	E	T	A			
B	E	E	N	A	T			H	Y	M	N	
O	N		S	T	A	R		A	S		N	O
R	O	D		E	T	H	A	N		T	A	I
D	U	O		R	I	O	T	S		A	S	S
E	G	G	S		O	D	E		A	L	O	E
R	H	E	A		N	A	D		M	E	N	D

20

T	O	W		B	R	A	Y		S	P	A	T
O	N	E		L	A	T	E		T	A	R	E
P	O	T	T	A	G	E		J	O	N	A	N
		U	S	E		D	U	N	G			
S	P	O	R	T		R	A	M	E	S	E	S
T	O	W	N		A	S	P	S		M	E	
O	I	L		P	A	T	H	S		D	I	E
R	N		C	A	G	E		A	R	M	S	
E	T	E	R	N	A	L		T	R	Y	S	T
	H	A	I	R		C	A	B				
S	T	U	N	T		G	A	L	A	T	I	A
A	I	D	E		B	A	K	E		I	R	U
M	E	S	S		E	Y	E	S		N	I	L

23

R	E	V	E	N	G	E		A	R	O	S	E
A	D	O	R	A	I	M		S	E	B	A	T
S	E	W		E	B	B		S	P	A	I	N
E	R	S	E		E	A	R		O	L	L	A
		L	O		L	I	A	R				
P	L	A	I	N		M	O	N	T	H	L	Y
I	O	D		I	F		T	O		O	P	E
T	W	O	F	O	L	D		D	I	A	N	A
		A	N	E	R		E	D				
F	L	A	T		D	O	R		E	B	E	D
O	A	T	H	S		P	I	E		O	D	E
A	L	O	E	S		S	T	R	A	N	G	E
M	A	M	R	E		Y	E	A	R	N	E	D

21

W	A	G		S	O	L	D		V	O	I	D
A	G	E		E	V	E	R		O	N	C	E
N	E	R		T	E	M	A		W	O	E	S
T	E	A	R		R	U	I	N	S			
		E	A		E	N	D		B	D	A	
C	A	B	R	I	L	L	A		B	E	O	R
A	L	L	U	R	E		G	A	L	E	E	D
M	O	O	N		N	E	E	S	I	N	G	S
P	E	W		E	T	A		A	N			
		A	D	I	S	H		D	I	R	T	
T	O	M	B		L	I	E	N		D	O	R
O	V	A	L		E	L	A	H		O	D	E
P	A	R	E		S	Y	R	A		L	E	E

24

T	H	E		B	A	L	D		S	H	E	D
O	I	L		A	S	E	R		H	E	R	E
I	R	I		G	A	D	A	R	E	N	E	S
L	E	S			V	O	W					
	A	M	I		B	E	D		M	U	G	
T	A	B	I	T	H	A			I	R	U	
O	D	E	D		E	A	T		U	S	E	S
T	I	T		L	O	A	D	E	T	H		
E	T	H		A	H	I		T	O	R		
	O	W	E					A	H	A		
R	E	F	R	E	S	H	E	D		B	A	R
A	C	R	E		E	A	S	E		L	I	E
J	O	A	B		D	Y	E	D		E	R	A

25

```
LOTHE █ POLICY
OPHIR █ AMASHAI
NEOMA █ PETIOLE
GNU █ BEG █ SKEE
LEG █ SERAH █ ESE
ESHBAN █ SEA █
ATTAI █ BRAKE
█ DNA █ TEMPER
RAM █ TIBER █ ORE
EBAC █ LIE █ LNC
ARGOMEN █ SPLIT
MAMMATE █ EMOTE
█ MARTHA █ EASED
```

28

```
POSER █ GRAPES
ARETAS █ REPENT
PATTEN █ EATERY
ATTE █ ARAM █ PAL
WOE █ FRET █ SEGO
█ RELIEF █ BIDE
█ ENSUEIT █
█ WAVE █ SNAZZY
MANY █ HEMS █ UEL
ETA █ BODE █ BRAE
CEIBAS █ SYRIAN
CRADLE █ HEREND
ASHIMA █ WELDS
```

26

```
█ NAMES █ SHED
RESORT █ LAVEER
HAGGAI █ ANGOLA
ERA █ SLANG █ DIK
SERF █ LID █ LAKE
ARDON █ JEHORAM
█ NAHARAI █
PALTIEL █ SNOWY
ENOS █ IOD █ SHOE
RIB █ AGNUS █ MLS
ISAIAH █ REPAVE
LETOUT █ SIEGES
█ ENNS █ TREES
```

29

```
HAM █ SLIP █ SIDE
OVA █ PATE █ ENON
WALKEDST █ ATAD
█ INNS █ ISLE █
█ SCOT █ UTTERED
SHIP █ TRIEDMEI
OEO █ ARGON █ ERE
FOURTEEN █ EDIT
ALSOAND █ FADE
█ NINA █ FURL █
FEEL █ IDLENESS
EASE █ LEAL █ TEA
DRSD █ SOWS █ HAY
```

27

```
█ ETHAN █ CHODE
STRIPE █ OOLITE
WHITHERSOEVER
ANUS █ DUET █ ERR
NAN █ DENY █ ERNE
█ NEWEST █ EASED
█ HATHHIS █
TIRED █ EARTHY
ENAN █ OWSE █ OES
NCV █ ACAD █ AMLE
THIRSTYORIOLE
HESTIA █ NASION
█ SHEAL █ ENDOW
```

30

```
SAT █ OHAD █ ARAM
ELI █ RACA █ BERA
ESTEEMED █ SPAN
DOINGS █ OLEO █
█ DOTE █ INRE
ALL █ NEGLECTED
SEAS █ REI █ EELY
COMPASSED █ DSO
█ NEON █ TIED █
█ NUTS █ NUANCE
NETS █ TATTLERS
FREE █ ACHE █ BOP
LIDS █ BEER █ SPY
```

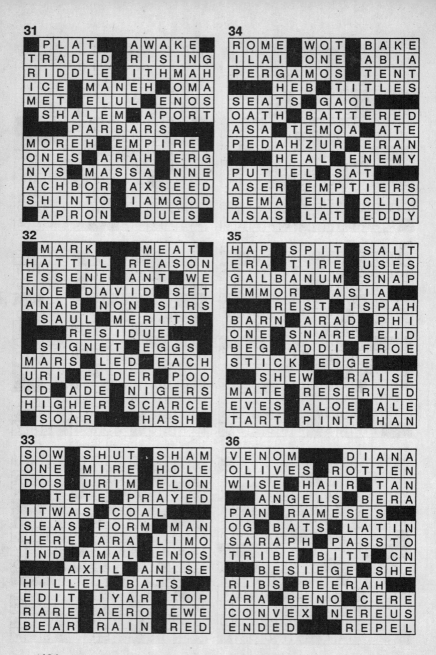

31

```
 P L A T     A W A K E
T R A D E D   R I S I N G
R I D D L E   I T H M A H
I C E   M A N E H   O M A
M E T   E L U L   E N O S
  S H A L E M   A P O R T
      P A R B A R S
M O R E H   E M P I R E
O N E S   A R A H   E R G
N Y S   M A S S A   N N E
A C H B O R   A X S E E D
S H I N T O   I A M G O D
  A P R O N     D U E S
```

34

```
R O M E   W O T   B A K E
I L A I   O N E   A B I A
P E R G A M O S   T E N T
    H E B   T I T L E S
S E A T S   G A O L
O A T H   B A T T E R E D
A S A   T E M O A   A T E
P E D A H Z U R   E R A N
    H E A L   E N E M Y
P U T I E L   S A T
A S E R   E M P T I E R S
B E M A   E L I   C L I O
A S A S   L A T   E D D Y
```

32

```
  M A R K     M E A T
H A T T I L   R E A S O N
E S S E N E   A N T   W E
N O E   D A V I D   S E T
A N A B   N O N   S I R S
  S A U L   M E R I T S
    R E S I D U E
  S I G N E T   E G G S
M A R S   L E D   E A C H
U R I   E L D E R   P O O
C D   A D E   N I G E R S
H I G H E R   S C A R C E
  S O A R     H A S H
```

35

```
H A P   S P I T   S A L T
E R A   T I R E   U S E S
G A L B A N U M   S N A P
E M M O R     A S I A
    R E S T   I S P A H
B A R N   A R A D   P H I
O N E   S N A R E   E I D
B E G   A D D I   F R O E
S T I C K   E D G E
  S H E W     R A I S E
M A T E   R E S E R V E D
E V E S   A L O E   A L E
T A R T   P I N T   H A N
```

33

```
S O W   S H U T   S H A M
O N E   M I R E   H O L E
D O S   U R I M   E L O N
    T E T E   P R A Y E D
I T W A S   C O A L
S E A S   F O R M   M A N
H E R E   A R A   L I M O
I N D   A M A L   E N O S
    A X I L   A N I S E
H I L L E L   B A T S
E D I T   I Y A R   T O P
R A R E   A E R O   E W E
B E A R   R A I N   R E D
```

36

```
V E N O M     D I A N A
O L I V E S   R O T T E N
W I S E   H A I R   T A N
    A N G E L S   B E R A
P A N   R A M E S E S
O G   B A T S   L A T I N
S A R A P H   P A S S T O
T R I B E   B I T T   C N
    B E S I E G E   S H E
R I B S   B E E R A H
A R A   B E N O   C E R E
C O N V E X   N E R E U S
E N D E D     R E P E L
```

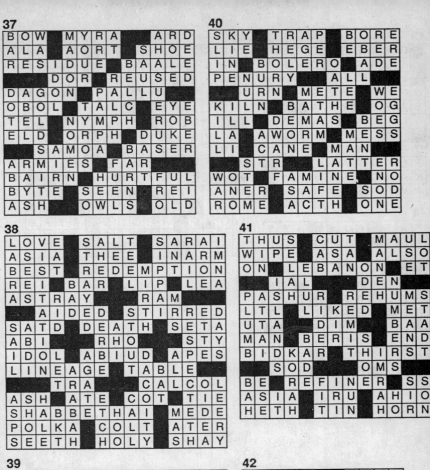

37

```
B O W   M Y R A     A R D
A L A   A O R T   S H O E
R E S I D U E   B A A L E
    D O R   R E U S E D
D A G O N   P A L L U
O B O L   T A L C   E Y E
T E L   N Y M P H   R O B
E L D   O R P H   D U K E
  S A M O A   B A S E R
A R M I E S   F A R
B A I R N   H U R T F U L
B Y T E   S E E N   R E I
A S H     O W L S   O L D
```

40

```
S K Y   T R A P   B O R E
L I E   H E G E   E B E R
I N   B O L E R O   A D E
P E N U R Y     A L L
    U R N   M E T E   W E
K I L N   B A T H E   O G
I L L   D E M A S   B E G
L A   A W O R M   M E S S
L I   C A N E   M A N
    S T R     L A T T E R
W O T   F A M I N E   N O
A N E R   S A F E   S O D
R O M E   A C T H   O N E
```

38

```
L O V E   S A L T   S A R A I
A S I A   T H E E   I N A R M
B E S T   R E D E M P T I O N
R E I   B A R   L I P   L E A
A S T R A Y     R A M
  A I D E D   S T I R R E D
S A T D   D E A T H   S E T A
A B I     R H O     S T Y
I D O L   A B I U D   A P E S
L I N E A G E   T A B L E
  T R A     C A L C O L
A S H   A T E   C O T   T I E
S H A B B E T H A I   M E D E
P O L K A   C O L T   A T E R
S E E T H   H O L Y   S H A Y
```

41

```
T H U S   C U T   M A U L
W I P E   A S A   A L S O
O N   L E B A N O N   E T
    I A L     D E N
P A S H U R   R E H U M S
L T L   L I K E D   M E T
U T A   D I M   B A A
M A N   B E R I S   E N D
B I D K A R   T H I R S T
  S O D     O M S
B E   R E F I N E R   S S
A S I A   I R U   A H I O
H E T H   T I N   H O R N
```

39

```
S A R O N   G A B A   E B A L
A R E L I   O N E S   L E G O
R E P E N T I N G S   E G A D
C A R   T O L A   E S C A P E
    O P H E L   S M I T T E N
B A B E L S   D E B T
I T A L Y   B A A L H A N A N
T E T E   B E L L Y   G E B A
E R E T H I S M S   C A G E Y
    A L E A   W H I L E S
H E A R E S T   D I A N E
A I L E T H   F I N N   C A D
S K I N   A B U N D A N T L Y
T O A D   N I L E   A N E L E
E N N S   S O L D   N E D E R
```

42

```
L A B A N     W A L K
E L E V E N   I L A I
D O   A S A   L O S S
G N U   T I L L E T H
E Z R A   L I E
S O I L S   P T E R O
    T O E   H A U L
P A R E N T S   R E I
O M A R   A L A   F V
C A R E   M A R Q U E
O D E D     V A U L T
```

43

	G	A	T	E	S		G	U	S	H
	I	S	A	A	C		O	L	E	O
	L	A	T	C	H		D	A	W	N
U	G	H		H	I	S	S	I	N	G
S	A	E	S		Z	I	A			
A	L	L	O	W		N	I	S	A	N
		L	O	T		D	A	D	O	
D	E	V	O	T	E	E		L	O	D
E	L	I	M		A	M	O	U	R	
K	A	N	O		R	I	A	T	A	
A	M	E	N		S	A	T	E	M	

44

F	A	T		G	A	S		A	B	I
I	R	I		L	U	C	I	F	E	R
G	E	N	E	A	L	O	G	I	E	S
		G	A	D		R	A	T	H	
F	E	L	T		I	C	L		I	N
A	X	E		A	S	H		E	V	E
R	E		A	S	A		D	U	E	T
	C	A	N	A		U	R	N		
M	U	L	T	I	P	L	Y	I	N	G
I	T	S	S	A	I	L		C	U	E
D	E	O		H	P	A		E	N	T

45

G	E	R	A		P	L	A	N	T		A	T	E	N
A	R	A	N		L	A	V	E	R		F	R	E	I
P	R	I	E		A	D	A	M	I		T	U	R	N
E	O	S		A	T	E		O	M	S		M	I	T
D	R	E	A	M	E	D			M	I	Z	P	E	H
		H	O	S		A	R	E	N	A				
J	O	N	A	S		A	L	A	S		R	A	C	A
O	V	E	R		S	L	A	N	T		E	B	A	L
B	A	T	H		I	M	R	I		S	T	I	P	E
	E	T	H	A	M		S	E	A					
H	A	L	L	O	O			S	H	I	N	E	T	H
E	L	I		E	N	T		O	E	R		A	H	I
W	O	M	B		A	R	G	U	E		A	T	A	D
E	N	O	S		N	I	E	S	T		M	E	N	E
R	E	S	T		D	A	T	E	S		I	R	K	S